UPCOMING AND RECENT RELEASES FROM THOMSON EXECUTIVE PRESS

CREATING CUSTOMER VALUE: THE PATH TO SUSTAINABLE COMPETITIVE ADVANTAGE

by Earl Naumann

The definitive source for the new business paradigm of customer value. This book shows you why business must go beyond product quality and integrate customers throughout their decision-making processes. Includes case studies from Baldrige Award winners such as Motorola, Hewlett-Packard, and Xerox.

Packaged with Naumann's book is an exciting new CD-ROM by the Mescon Multimedia Group that allows you to work with the principles of *Creating Customer Value* in a convenient, hands-on format. *Customer Driven Companies* includes over 55 minutes of instructional video, a self-scoring Baldrige questionnaire, and full search capabilities.

CUSTOMER SATISFACTION MEASUREMENT AND MANAGEMENT: USING THE VOICE OF THE CUSTOMER

by Earl Naumann and Kathleen Giel

You *can* survive ever-increasing levels of customer expectation. This book shows you, step-by-step, how to implement a customer satisfaction measurement and management program that permeates every level of your company, so that you may thrive as a truly customer-driven company. Includes a free demo disk for *Corporate Pulse*™—a revolutionary diagnostic software program developed by The Praxis Group.

REENGINEERING S___ __DE: MANA___ IN_

by ___

Thi_ _____ ___ ___ implications of r____ ___ __ _ow to survive and prosper in a restructured work environment. You'll learn how to manage people, as well as your career, smoothly and confidently in today's turbulent corporate terrain. Self-examination quizzes and checklists are among the tools DuBrin provides to help you grasp the new leadership protocol.

BUILDING COMMUNITY: THE HUMAN SIDE OF WORK

by George Manning, Kent Curtis, and Steve McMillen

Building community between people is the focus of this engaging book. It is written for the work setting, but is applicable to any situation where communication, teamwork, and valuing diversity are important. This book uses applications and experiential learning to teach skills.

THE LEGAL PROFESSION: IS IT FOR YOU?

by Wayne L. Anderson and Marilyn J. Headrick

Helps those considering a legal profession by presenting an overview of what is required, the choices available, and common obstacles to a profession in law.

TEP

5101 Madison Road
Cincinnati, OH 45227
800/328-0500 voice
800/585-0880 fax

We welcome your inquiries about these innovative titles. Thomson Executive Press is also ready to help you address your organization's training needs through customized programs. Give us a call.

GREENING BUSINESS

Profiting the Corporation and the Environment

PAUL SHRIVASTAVA

THOMSON EXECUTIVE PRESS
A Division of South-Western College Publishing

Sponsoring Editor: Jim Sitlington
Production Editor: Holly Terry
Development: Custom Editorial Productions, Inc.
Production House: Trejo Production
Internal Design: Ellen Pettengell
Cover Design: Joseph M. Devine
Marketing Manager: Stephen E. Momper

Copyright © 1996
by THOMSON EXECUTIVE PRESS
Cincinnati, Ohio

I(T)P
International Thomson Publishing
Thomson Executive Press (a division of South-Western College Publishing) is
an ITP Company. The trademark ITP is used under license.

Library of Congress Cataloging-in-Publication Data

Shrivastava, Paul.
     Greening business: profiting the corporation and the environment / by
     Paul Shrivastava.
          p. cm.
     Includes bibliographical references and index.
     1. Industrial management--Environmental aspects. 2. Sustainable
     development. 3. Environmental policy. 4. Industrial management--
     Environmental aspects--Case studies.
     I. Title.
     HD30.255.S47 1996
     658.4'08dc20   94-43418
                                                                 CIP

     ISBN: 0-538-84452-3 (alk. paper)

1 2 3 4 5 MT 9 8 7 6 5

Printed in the United States of America

 This book is printed on acid-free paper that meets Environmental
Protection Agency standards for recycled paper. It is also printed
using vegetable-based (non-metal) ink.

FOR CLAUDIA AND KYLE
AND THEIR GENERATION,
WITH HOPES THAT THE GREENING OF BUSINESS
WILL IMPROVE THEIR LIVES AND ENVIRONMENT.

Acknowledgments

I am most grateful for the many conversations at Bucknell University that have shaped parts of this book. The idea for it originated from discussions with the University's environmental faculty. Bucknell also provided an ideal interdisciplinary environment for me to learn about the managerial, economic, sociological, geological, religious, and technological aspects of our environmental problems.

During the 1992–93 academic year, President Gary Sojka initiated a unique intellectual endeavor, the President's Forum on the Environmental Initiative. This program brought to our campus such renowned environmental scholars as Thomas Berry, Barry Commoner, Robert F. Kennedy, Jr., Lynn Margulies, and James McNeil. Discussions with them provided focus for the book. I am thankful to these speakers and the Bucknell community for educating me.

For research interviews, access to company publications and documents, and for sharing their opinions, I thank managers in my sample companies. I am particularly grateful to Dr. Deborah Anderson and George Carpenter of Procter & Gamble, Mitch Curren and members of the Green Team of Ben & Jerry's Homemade Ice Creams, Inc., Dr. David Wheeler of The Body Shop, and Patrick Carlson of Loblaw International Merchants.

For reading complete drafts of this book I want to thank Ray Aldag (University of Wisconsin–Madison), Carolyn Egri (Simon

Fraser University), Kath Giel (Boise Cascade Company), Donald Milner (Edgewood Capital Corporation), and Ian Mitroff (University of Southern California). My students at Bucknell read individual chapters and gave me valuable feedback. Philip Elliot provided able assistance in researching the case studies. Thanks, too, to Jim Sitlington of Thomson Executive Press for his sustained enthusiasm, his entrepreneurial drive, and unflagging pursuit of this project, and for giving the very able support of his editorial, production, and marketing teams.

My family has put up with my book writings before. But while I was writing this one, I was also editing another and proofreading a third. The consequences of such poor schedule I would not wish on my enemies; they could be endured only by true friends. I thank them for recognizing me whenever I surfaced from my "dungeon" office. For feeding me, loving me, and not disowning me by the end of the process, I am profoundly grateful to my wife, Michelle Cooper.

Finally, it is customary to accept responsibility for any errors that remain in the book. With all the help that I received, I would like to fantasize that there aren't any. But if you find some, then I want to thank you, the reader, in advance for bringing them to my attention.

Paul Shrivastava
Lewisburg, Pennsylvania

Preface

You picked up this book because you are already aware of the environmental problems facing the world. You are also environmentally conscientious, but find yourself working for an organization that does not yet have a great environmental record.

To provoke action within giant and often bureaucratic corporations, we need compelling logic and incentives. The logic for action argued in this book is simple. It says that environmentally responsible action is as good for the bottom line, for employee welfare, and for the long-term survival of corporations as it is necessary for resolving the Earth's ecological problems. Corporations should green themselves not simply to be ethical or to yield to political pressures. Instead, as the following chapters show, greening today is a competitive, ecological, economic, political, and social necessity.

To move your organization toward environmentally responsible behavior, you need first to understand the scale of the problem and *why* such change is necessary. You need to know *who* is environmentally responsible, and *how* other companies are becoming environmental leaders. Finally, you should know *what* you can change within your own organization.

This book shows why it is critical for corporations to deal with environmental issues. In Part I, I argue that corporate greening is necessary, and not simply because it is the right thing to do. Instead, it is a matter of long-term economic and physical survival (Chapter 2). It can provide competitive advantage, be an aid to total quality management, and help companies to expand into global markets (Chapter 3). Finally, greening is a social, political, and ethical necessity (Chapter 4).

Part II is the empirical base of the book. It describes green companies that have achieved financial success on a global scale by making environmental responsiveness a cornerstone of their strategies. Companies in the sample are The Body Shop (Chapter 5), Proctor & Gamble, Inc. (Chapter 6), Loblaw International Merchants, Inc. (Chapter 7), Ben & Jerry's Homemade Ice Creams, Inc. (Chapter 8), The Volvo Car Company (Chapter 9) and The 3M Company (Chapter 10). I discuss their environmental programs and efforts to green themselves. Chapter 11 examines the Japanese approach to greening.

Part III provides an organizational framework linking all parts of the corporation to environmental actions (Chapter 12). This framework also shows how firms can simultaneously become more productive and competitive. Chapter 13 discusses tools and techniques for environmental management. Chapter 14 takes a speculative look at the green corporation of the future. It discusses second-order greening, in which companies are compatible with bioregional resources and community demands.

Contents

PART *I*

WHY GREEN: THE LOGIC FOR GREENING

*T*he first section of the book lays out the basic framework for the book. Chapter 1 describes ecological issues facing corporations in this decade and the coming century. These issues present both problems and opportunities for companies. Chapter 2 discusses one possible solution in the form of ecologically sustainable economic development implemented through ecologically sustainable corporations.

Chapters 3 and 4 argue that there are many compelling business reasons for greening your company. Ecologically sustainable strategies can help improve our environment and preserve ecological resources. They can also improve your company's competitive position, enhance total quality management, and help your company to expand globally.

Greening can improve your company's public image as a socially responsible company. Finally, with new regulations and public pressures for ecological improvements, there may be no alternative to greening. Proactive and systematic greening will eventually be good both for the environment and the bottom line.

In summary, this section gives compelling reasons for greening your company. But if you are already convinced about this need, you may want to skip to Part II of the book, which describes how companies are moving toward ecological sustainability. In The tools and processes for greening your company are provided in Part III. There are special checklists for greening different tasks and functions that you can use immediately to initiate action.

The Corporate Environmental Challenge

It is six a.m. on an April morning in the year 2030. You wake up, shower, and apply RayShield ultraviolet protection lotion. You drink a cup of decaffeinated coffee. You then put on your gas mask and start the 90-minute, eight-mile commute to work at the World Industrial Park.

On the congested highway, your car computer detours you into a 10-mile loop. The car's chemical sensors then add another 10-mile detour to avoid a chemical plume accidentally released by a truck on the highway.

SMOG CAR

Source: Stan Eales, *Earthtoons*, Warner Books, copyright 1991. Reprinted with permission from the publisher.

You pass an entombed nuclear plant. Here, a group of protesters with banners and placards are opposing government efforts to remove spent nuclear fuel.

At the Park gate, you pass voice and palm print security sensors. An elevator lifts your car into a solar charge slot on Level 46. You take an escalator to your office building. There you go through a decontamination chamber wearing a "dungeon suit." The suit protects you and your fellow workers from mutual immune system invasions.

The world population is now 11 billion. Most people live in megalopolises stretching over multi-city corridors along the Sunbelt states from California to Florida. The world has "resolved" the ecological crises caused by ozone depletion, global warming, toxic wastes, and air pollution.

The earth still exists and life continues. However, the price of survival is a continual mass movement of ecological refugees. There are many armed conflicts over natural resources. The average life expectancy around the world is declining, as a result of increased immune-system disorders. Personal protection and security are the primary concern, in work, meals, entertainment, movement, and creative expression.

You may think this is a fantasy. It is not. This scenario is a composite of situations that already exist in different parts of the world today. Industrial processes of the past two centuries have profoundly disturbed the billion-year-old ecological equilibrium of the earth.

Three fundamental realizations mark our corporate understanding of these ecological changes:

1. There is a ground swell of public awareness and support for environmental protection. Many companies have acknowledged this, and are engaging in corporate environmentalism.

2. In a post-industrial society, managing risks to the environment from technology will be the central problem facing corporations.
3. The root cause of current problems with the environment is a pattern of industrial growth that cannot be sustained by our ecology.

This chapter develops these three themes as a way of looking at the environmental challenges facing corporations today and into the next century.

I use the colorful term "greening" to capture the many responses of companies to environmental concerns. The notion of greening allows us to sum up a broad range of concerns about both the natural and human environments of companies. It covers issues of environmental protection, human health, conservation of resources, technological risks, and worker and customer safety. Companies need to integrate these activities into a coherent strategy of environmental management, which I call "greening."

In our current "post-industrial" society economic production is not confined to traditional industrial sectors. It occurs mostly in service and high-tech sectors that are dynamic and volatile. Finance, production, and markets are global. Economic growth cannot be unlinked from degradation of the environment.

The Ground Swell of Environmentalism

We are witnessing a level of grass-roots environmental action without precedent. Communities across the world are more conscious than ever before of local environmental problems. In the United States, communities are responding to such problems in both positive and negative ways. They are engaged in recycling programs, environmental education, land and marine conservation, tree plantings, and wildlife restoration.

At the same time, an aggressive "not in my backyard" (NIMBY) attitude has led more than 7,000 communities to resist local development of undesirable facilities. It is nearly impossible to get permission to build new landfills. There is widespread opposition to hazardous waste incinerators. Communities frequently resist even job-creating new industry, urban development, and highways.

Publics around the world are aware of environmental problems and business responsibility for them. A survey done by the Gallup International Institute in 1992 showed wide agreement that the world environment is in a fairly or very bad state and that business contributes to environmental problems, and wide support for environmental protection over economic growth.

Business corporations, the main engines of industrial growth, face real pressures to respond to these environmental concerns. Customers are demanding safer and cleaner production facilities and waste-recycling programs. Employees are demanding safer and healthier work conditions. Governments are legislating thousands of environmental protection measures each year. Membership in environmental conservation groups, such as the World Wildlife Federation, the Sierra Club, and Greenpeace International, has more than doubled in the past decade. And the media are giving strong voice to these demands.

The broad awareness of the seriousness of environmental problems has prompted corporate action. Many companies are introducing internal programs to make themselves more environmentally responsive, and to develop pro-environment attitudes, values, and postures within the firm.

TECHNO-ENVIRONMENTAL RISK MANAGEMENT IN POST-INDUSTRIAL SOCIETY

The technological and industrial progress of the past two centuries has truly been miraculous. In advanced industrial societies it has brought unimagined advantages. This industrial cornucopia has been the source of lavish modern benefits and conveniences. Technological advancement has revolutionized agriculture, medicine, transportation, and communication. It has raised life expectancy and standards of living worldwide. It has promised unending and ever-expanding prosperity for all.

This technological optimism of the past is now being tempered. The environmental degradation that technology has brought is raising basic concerns about industrial growth. The environmental risks unleashed by this growth have become acute enough to warrant world attention.

For corporations, the key issue is to understand the relationship of wealth to risk. Risks are a by-product of producing wealth. This was true even in pre-industrial societies, although then the risks were very small. Economic activities were smaller in scale and did not use broadly hazardous technologies. In industrial societies, risks were viewed as side effects or "externalities" of production. Governments were responsible for dealing with them. And the public, via government, imposed taxes that absorbed the costs of dealing with them.

In the current post-industrial society, the relationship of wealth and risk is reversed. The risks are greater, more harmful, geographically more pervasive, longer term, and more difficult to measure. They are often unknown, and easily cross national and other social boundaries, having a negative impact on the quality of life in communities all over the world. Risks are a key aspect of just about everything we do. As Ulrich Beck has said, the post-industrial society is a "risk society"—a society in which all economic and social activity is accompanied by significant risks.

The nature of modern risk is different from the risks of earlier eras. Pre-industrial societies risked disease, pestilence, and natural disasters. Blame for these things could be externalized to God or nature. Modern risks are the result of human decisions—economic, social, technological, and organizational.

Environmental and technological risks are created unintentionally, by organizations and institutions that are supposed to control and manage them. But traditional approaches to risk management have failed. And the people affected by these failures must then try to deal with large, impersonal, and often inaccessible corporations and government agencies. They are frustrated by their limited access and their inability to influence risk-creating decisions. This has made them skeptical about such risk-related institutions as corporations, government agencies, and even scientific bodies.

The public's negative perception of technological risks to the environment is heightened by frequent high-profile industrial accidents such as the Chernobyl nuclear power plant explosion, the *Exxon Valdez* oil spill, and the Bhopal chemical-plant disaster. These perceptions are not always consistent with the actual damage done. For example, 10 times the oil spilled by *Exxon Valdez* is poured down sewers and into waterways each year. The public does not complain about this. Yet, the mega-accidents act as powerful symbols of technological risk. They are lightning rods that focus the public's negative perceptions about technology, and elicit resistance to technological expansion.

Technological and environmental risks pose new challenges for corporate managers and public policy officials. It is not sufficient that corporations only optimize such production variables as profits, productivity, jobs, and growth. Corporations must also manage such risk variables as product harm, pollution, waste, resources, technological hazards, and worker and public safety. This is not just an expansion of the management agenda. As pointed out by Vice President Al Gore, it implies shifting the focus of management attention from production to risk.

An important reason for the emergence of risk as a central variable in modernization is the ecologically unsustainable pattern of industrialization that the world has pursued over the past century. Energy-intensive, resource-intensive, and pollution-creating industrialization has brought many ecosystems to the brink of crisis.

THE EFFECTS OF INDUSTRIAL GROWTH ON ECOLOGY

Industrialization has been a central feature of modern societies. It has brought enormous economic growth, technological advancement, and social prosperity to nearly a quarter of the world's population. Indeed, the success of industrialization has been so dazzling that, until recently, we failed to notice the burden that industrial activities place on the ecosystem.

Industrialization is characterized by expanding technological products and production, large-scale production systems, energy- and capital-intensive industries, and expanding urban settlements. It is based on the assumption that we have unlimited natural resources available and that the earth's capacity to act as a sink for industrially produced wastes is inexhaustible.

Slowly but surely it is dawning on us that industrial production, products, wastes, accidents, and the unrestrained use of natural resources have caused multiple environmental problems. Now these problems are reaching levels where they threaten the stability and survival of earth's ecosystems. Corporations that own and manage industrial systems face enormous environmental challenges in coming years. These challenges can be understood only by examining the links between environmental problems and corporate activities.

In the next 40 years the world population will double from the current 5.5 billion to nearly 11 billion. The current level of production (about $20 trillion) will have to be increased five to 30 times simply to provide basic amenities to this increased population. This is clearly ecologically unsustainable, given current technologies and resource-use strategies.

At current rates of use, natural resources are being depleted faster than they can be renewed. World oil supplies could be exhausted in about 30 years. Most other mineral resources could be depleted within the next century. The extraction of natural resources and expansion of human development are destroying large tracts of forests and natural habitats, and extinguishing over 10,000 species of life each year. In the United States, many forest-product companies practice "sustainable yield" forestry. They plant up to six trees for each one harvested. This strategy more than compensates for the lumber removed, but does not replace the biological diversity of the original forests.

Despite our best attempts to make products safe and harmless, they can cause unintended but severe harm. Chlorofluorocarbons (CFCs) serve as refrigerants, industrial solvents and an ingredient for Styrofoam plastics. When released into the atmosphere they destroy the earth's protective ozone shield. Periodically, holes in the ozone layer appear over the North and South Poles for several months each year, allowing excess radiation to enter the earth's atmosphere. In the United States, this results in increased skin cancers, cataracts—and a crop loss of 6 to 7 percent. Ironically, when CFCs were introduced in the 1950s, they were considered safer for the environment and human health than the more dangerous and flammable refrigerants in use then.

The overuse of agricultural chemicals is another example. Repeated use of these chemicals weakens the soil. Pesticides enter the food chain and harm humans and animals who consume the food. Careless and unprotected use of pesticides poisons more than 500,000 persons annually. The recent scare involving excess quantities of Alar growth hormone in apples exemplifies how susceptible we are to chemicals in our foods.

In some cases, harm results from a lack of knowledge about hazards, or the lack of safety and environmental-protection measures. Johns Manville (asbestos maker) and the Chisso Company of Japan (which poured mercury waste into the Minamata Bay) did not fully understand the severe environmental and health hazards of their product- and waste-management activities. They continued to pollute the environment until they were forced to stop by court and government decisions.

Technological accidents have created environmental crises and corporate crises. The Three Mile Island nuclear power plant accident released minor amounts of radiation and did not immediately kill anyone. But it created a crisis of public confidence for Metropolitan Edison Company and its parent, General Public Utilities, Inc. It also halted the development of nuclear power in the United States for more than a decade. The Bhopal disaster at the Union Carbide Plant in India killed more than 3,000 people and injured more than 300,000. In the following eight years it resulted in the downsizing of Union Carbide to half its pre-accident size and led to many new regulations of the chemical industry around the world.

A major source of environmental pollution is the transportation of hazardous materials. The ocean oil spills of the *Exxon Valdez* (Prince William Sound, Alaska) and the *Amoco Cadiz* (off the French coast) exemplify the environmental damage that can be caused by transportation disasters. Government inspection of transportation safety is minimal. Less than 2 percent of container manufacturers and less than 1 percent of shipping facilities are inspected each year. The time devoted to safety inspections—by the U.S. Coast Guard, Federal Aviation Administration, Federal Highway Administration, and Materials Transportation Bureau together—declined in the 1980s.

Hazardous industrial wastes are another common source of environmental crises. Stockpiles of wastes from the oil, chemicals, construction, defense production, electronics, metals and mining, nuclear power, pharmaceutical, paper, and pulp industries are contaminating land, water, and air. Many industrial facilities around the nation contain hazardous wastes buried on-site, without protection for the surrounding natural environment.

Companies and government guided by the Comprehensive Environmental Responsibility, Cleanup and Liability Act (Superfund) have started to clean up hazardous waste sites. But the cleanup effort is not up to the size of the problem. The Environmental Protection Agency (EPA), Office of Technology Assess-

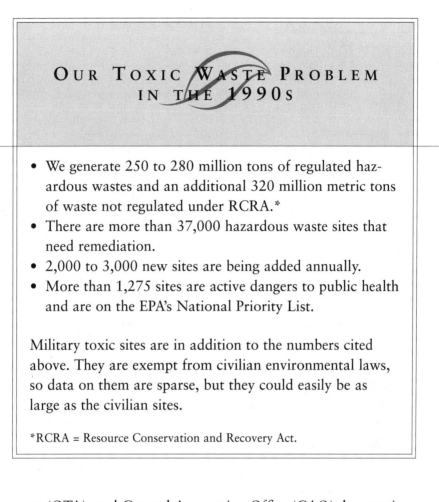

OUR TOXIC WASTE PROBLEM IN THE 1990s

- We generate 250 to 280 million tons of regulated hazardous wastes and an additional 320 million metric tons of waste not regulated under RCRA.*
- There are more than 37,000 hazardous waste sites that need remediation.
- 2,000 to 3,000 new sites are being added annually.
- More than 1,275 sites are active dangers to public health and are on the EPA's National Priority List.

Military toxic sites are in addition to the numbers cited above. They are exempt from civilian environmental laws, so data on them are sparse, but they could easily be as large as the civilian sites.

*RCRA = Resource Conservation and Recovery Act.

ment (OTA), and General Accounting Office (GAO), have estimated the cost of cleanup for these sites—between $50 billion and $150 billion. Actual funding for cleanup (under Superfund Amendment and Reauthorization Act, SARA) was $1.6 billion for the 1982–86 period, and $5 billion for 1986–91, an average of $600 million per year. It is not surprising that even after a decade of cleanup efforts, there are more hazardous waste sites today than ever before.

Power plants burning fossil fuels, emissions from chemical, paper, and cement factories, automobile exhaust, and unintended leaks of harmful chemicals all pour pollution into the at-

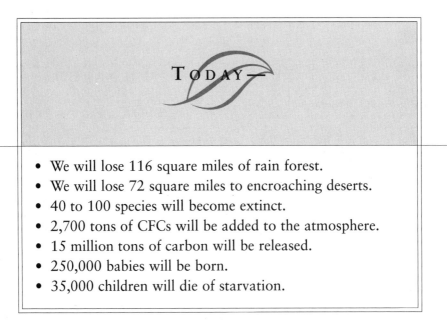

TODAY—

- We will lose 116 square miles of rain forest.
- We will lose 72 square miles to encroaching deserts.
- 40 to 100 species will become extinct.
- 2,700 tons of CFCs will be added to the atmosphere.
- 15 million tons of carbon will be released.
- 250,000 babies will be born.
- 35,000 children will die of starvation.

mosphere. In Mexico City, Los Angeles, London, New York City, São Paulo, Brazil, Lagos, Nigeria, and Tokyo, heavy air pollution is a public health crisis.

Worldwide emission of carbon products is about 5.5 billion tons per year. At the global level, air pollution from carbon dioxide and oxides of sulphur and nitrogen is suspected to cause acid rain, ozone depletion, and global warming—a long-term rise in the average temperature of the earth—by trapping heat in the earth's atmosphere. Global warming can in turn raise sea level, drowning large parts of currently inhabited lands, and cause changes in climate that are hostile to established patterns of world agriculture, animal farming, and human habitation.

Sulphur dioxide and nitrogen oxides emitted into the air by the burning of fossil fuels cause acid rain. The United States of America alone emits about 20 million tons of these gases each year. This makes up about 25 percent of world emissions of these substances. Acid rain caused by these chemicals has resulted in the destruction of forests, lakes, soil, and crops.

These environmental problems raise fundamental questions about corporate-environment relationships that urgently deserve the attention of corporate managers:

- Are today's corporations environmentally sustainable in the long run?
- How can they manage non-renewable natural resources to prevent their extinction?
- How can the health effects of industrial activities be controlled?
- How can worker and consumer health be protected?
- How can work safety and occupational hazards be reduced?
- How can public risks from corporate products and production systems be managed?
- How can industrialization and urbanization be made more friendly to the environment?

Environment, safety, health, and technological risks are moving to center stage of society's agenda. They are no longer marginal technical issues that can be passed down to lower levels in companies. They influence and are in turn influenced by a host of strategic, financial, human, organizational, social, and cultural factors. Top managers need to understand them and develop adequate responses to them.

THE ENVIRONMENTAL CHALLENGE FACING CORPORATIONS

The environmental challenge corporations face today is their complete changeover to forms that can be sustained by the environment. Corporations must seriously address the issues of safety, health, and environmental protection. Such greening will affect nearly all aspects of a company. It involves creating a new vision of what the company is and wants to be.

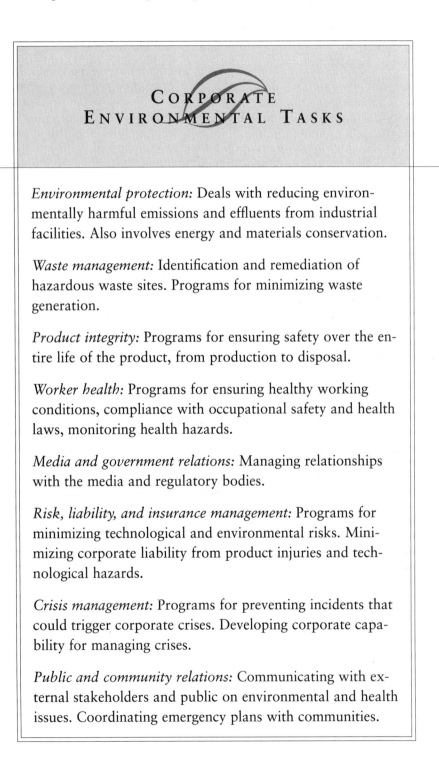

CORPORATE ENVIRONMENTAL TASKS

Environmental protection: Deals with reducing environmentally harmful emissions and effluents from industrial facilities. Also involves energy and materials conservation.

Waste management: Identification and remediation of hazardous waste sites. Programs for minimizing waste generation.

Product integrity: Programs for ensuring safety over the entire life of the product, from production to disposal.

Worker health: Programs for ensuring healthy working conditions, compliance with occupational safety and health laws, monitoring health hazards.

Media and government relations: Managing relationships with the media and regulatory bodies.

Risk, liability, and insurance management: Programs for minimizing technological and environmental risks. Minimizing corporate liability from product injuries and technological hazards.

Crisis management: Programs for preventing incidents that could trigger corporate crises. Developing corporate capability for managing crises.

Public and community relations: Communicating with external stakeholders and public on environmental and health issues. Coordinating emergency plans with communities.

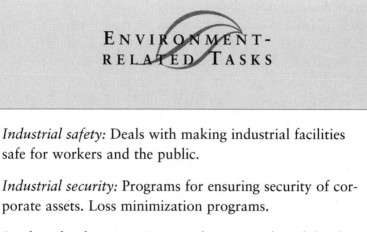

ENVIRONMENT-
RELATED TASKS

Industrial safety: Deals with making industrial facilities safe for workers and the public.

Industrial security: Programs for ensuring security of corporate assets. Loss minimization programs.

Product development: New product research and development, testing and launch.

Marketing: Product planning, sales, pricing, distribution, and promotion.

Total quality management: Programs for ensuring product quality.

Environmental, safety, and health concerns have already spawned many functional tasks within companies, such as are shown in the boxes on the next two pages.

While the lists in the boxes look impressive, they present several problems. First, many corporations do only a few of these tasks. Others do most of these tasks, but in a fragmented way and without coordination. Different groups located in different parts of the company do each task. Third, most companies do these tasks with a "regulatory compliance" mentality. They do the minimum necessary to satisfy regulations.

This compliance attitude and fragmentation misses a major opportunity for parlaying environmental tasks for competitive advantage. If organized as a comprehensive environmental

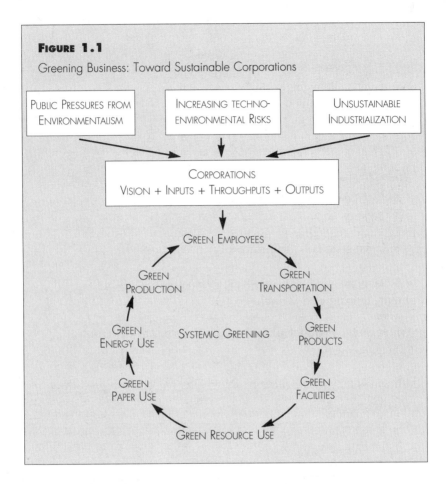

FIGURE 1.1

Greening Business: Toward Sustainable Corporations

PUBLIC PRESSURES FROM ENVIRONMENTALISM

INCREASING TECHNO-ENVIRONMENTAL RISKS

UNSUSTAINABLE INDUSTRIALIZATION

CORPORATIONS
VISION + INPUTS + THROUGHPUTS + OUTPUTS

GREEN EMPLOYEES

GREEN PRODUCTION

GREEN TRANSPORTATION

GREEN ENERGY USE

SYSTEMIC GREENING

GREEN PRODUCTS

GREEN PAPER USE

GREEN FACILITIES

GREEN RESOURCE USE

strategy, these tasks can save costs, enhance revenues and profits, and provide competitive advantage.

Corporations need to:

- Create new missions, goals and strategies.
- Conserve such inputs as energy and raw materials.
- Develop environmentally friendly products and packaging.
- Develop more efficient and cleaner production systems.
- Minimize and manage wastes and polluting emissions.
- Develop green organizational structures, systems, cultures, and competencies.

It's not going to be easy. Managers face formidable barriers to greening their companies—regulatory complications, structural roadblocks, limits on resources, lack of information, inadequate technologies, and no conceptual frameworks to help them achieve their greening goals. Managers also face the contradictory pressures of managing short-term profitability while striving for long-term environmental performance.

Few upper level managers in U.S. companies are experienced or trained in dealing with environmental problems. This is not surprising. Even until 1990, not a single major business school in the United States offered a comprehensive course in environmental management. Today, finally, several leading business schools are initiating such courses.

Ideas and techniques for achieving the tasks listed above form the bulk of this book. The arguments thus far are summarized in Figure 1.1.

Sustainable Development and Sustainable Corporations

We need to make no apology
For thinking about world ecology
For mere economics
Is stuff for the comics
Unless we can live with biology.

How can we achieve the facility
To encourage some sustainability
When all that it means
When it comes to our genes
Is to overexpand our virility.

To stop the extinction of species
We must do something with our faeces
And we have to relieve
The air that we breathe
Of the hot CO_2 that increases.

We need to do something in haste
About the production of waste
For if we do not
Then what have we got
But a world that is not to our taste.

KENNETH E. BOULDING
ECOLOGICAL ECONOMICS

Reprinted by permission from the publisher, Columbia University Press, copyright 1992.

Why should corporations bother about the natural environment? For long-term survival. Unrestrained economic and industrial growth have bestowed a grand standard of living on people in developed countries. Yet the survival of corporations and industries depends on the survival of earth's ecosystems. Only with corporate greening can corporations—the main engines of economic development—be made ecologically sustainable.

The population of the world has grown from 2.5 billion in 1950 to about 5.5 billion. (See Figure 2.1.) Each year, world population grows by 85 million people. Less than one-fourth of this population lives in affluent, industrialized Western countries. Yet, these countries produce and consume nearly three-fourths of world resources, and they generate nearly three-fourths of world pollution and waste.

The remaining three fourths of the world lives in developing countries. These people live in poverty. They do not have the resources to meet even their basic needs for food, clothing, and shelter. But they aspire to achieve the standards of living in developed countries. Yet, if developing countries achieved Western living standards through industrialization, every family in China and India would have a refrigerator and a car. That would produce enough CFCs and air pollution to cause catastrophic ozone loss and global warming. The earth's environment would be destroyed.

This situation becomes worse when we consider further growth in the world population. By 2030, it could double to about 11 billion. By then, 84 percent of the world would be living in developing countries. Just providing basic amenities would require increasing world production and energy use up to 30 times today's levels. The current level of production already places enormous strain on the environment. Imagine what a 30-fold increase in production would do! Imagine 30 times more pollution, 30 times more toxic wastes, 30 more Bhopals and Chernobyls.

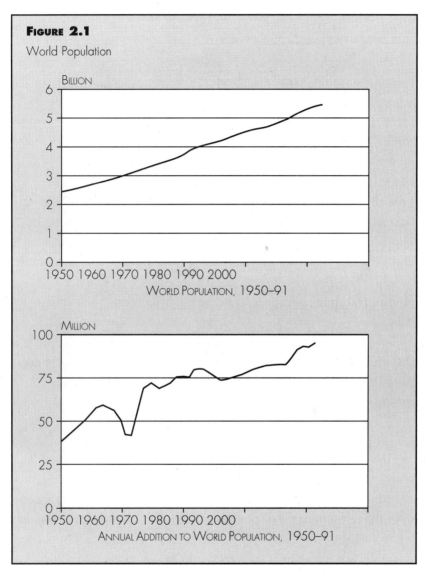

FIGURE 2.1

World Population

World Population, 1950–91

Annual Addition to World Population, 1950–91

Source: U.S. Census Bureau, as presented in L. Brown, C. Flavin, H. Kanes, Vital Signs, 1992: The Trends That Are Shaping Our Future. New York: W. W. Norton, 1992.

There are now well-recognized limits to conventional industrial growth. These limits arise from the finite availability of natural resources. In addition the natural environment has only limited ability to deal with pollution and degradation. Economic growth in the 21st century must be built on the idea of *environmentally sustainable development.* Sustainable development is development that is conscious of limits of the natural environment to support growth. It moderates the rate of use of natural resources, and attempts to renew these resources. It is development that does not jeopardize the ability of future generations to meet their own needs.

Sustainable development does not imply a halt in all economic growth—it asks only for halting *conventional* forms of growth. It questions growth strategies that are energy-intensive, that deplete nonrenewable resources, pollute the environment, and generate excessive amounts of toxic waste. It challenges corporations to create an alternative form of sustainable growth. Sustainable growth conserves and uses energy sensibly. It renews resources and preserves the environment. It minimizes waste.

The public and governments around the world are accepting the need for sustainable development strategies. This means corporations and economies can continue to grow only if they master strategies of sustainable development.

What Is Sustainable Development?

Sustainable development refers to a set of interrelated strategies to manage the impact of population growth on the environment and to ensure food security for the world population. On the resource side these strategies focus on managing ecosystem resources and creating an environmentally sound economy. In all these crucial tasks corporations have an important role to play.

Population Impacts

The total population and the rate of population growth in many countries is simply too high. It is far beyond what can be supported by existing environmental resources. Mass poverty and shortages of food, water, shelter, and hygienic living conditions are endemic in many developing countries. Sustainable development in these countries requires control of their exploding populations.

From an environmental perspective, population is not simply a developing-country problem. The impact of people on the environment is a complex issue. It depends not only on how many exist, but also on how they relate to their natural environment, their level of affluence, and what types of technology they use. Ehrlich and Ehrlich (1990) argue persuasively that

$$\text{Environmental Impact} = \text{Population} \times \text{Affluence} \times \text{Technology}$$

People in industrialized countries consume 30 to 80 times the energy and resources per capita consumed by people in developing countries.

As you can see, a large part of the population pressure on the natural environment comes from overconsumption in industrialized countries. Thus, managing the impact of population on the environment requires controlling consumption as well as population growth.

This has important implications for corporations. Historically, corporations have thrived on the emergence of consumer societies. They encouraged uncontrolled consumption through promotion and advertising. This has bred a consumerist, even anti-conservationist ethic in the population.

Sustainable development requires more controlled and thoughtful patterns of consumption. It calls for environmentally functional products and packaging. It requires cleaner and smaller-scale production systems. It means rethinking corporate promotion and advertising approaches.

Food Security

The problems of food security in rich industrial countries differ from those in poor developing countries. Food production in rich industrialized countries has increased tremendously. This is partly a result of irrigation, pesticides and fertilizers, and hybrid seeds. But the increase has come at the cost of degrading cultivated land and reducing the ecological diversity of cultivated crops. The consumption style of rich countries leads to waste, deliberate destruction, and underuse of food resources.

Today, we produce more food than is necessary to feed the world population. World grain production per person grew steadily till 1970, and has now leveled out. (See Figure 2.2.) Yet more people go without food each year, even though most countries subsidize and protect food production.

Developing countries lack land reforms, political stability, appropriate weather conditions, and efficient means of food production and distribution. Moreover, in the past 50 years their populations have doubled, resulting in large-scale food shortages. These countries face rampant malnutrition and mass starvation.

Sustainable development means dealing with the existing artificial imbalance in food distribution. Developing countries must provide economic and political incentives, land reforms, and protection to make small farmers and rural families economically viable. Restoring political stability is often a prerequisite for economic development. Industrialized countries must transfer surplus food stocks, at least during a short-term transition period, to prevent mass hunger.

Here again, corporations have a role to play because they control many parts of the food production and distribution chain. In industrialized countries, food production is under the control of the agricultural industry. Industrial processes involving plant genetics, pesticides, and fertilizers enhance agricultural productivity, but are ecologically harmful. There are fewer than a dozen grain-trading companies that control trade, prices, and movement of food across national borders. With so much power over food resources, these corporations are vital players in ensuring food security.

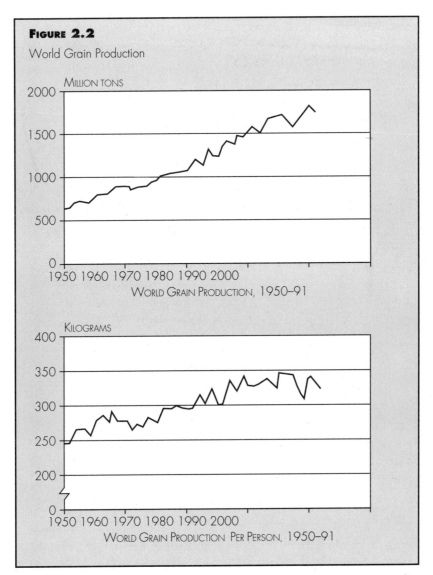

FIGURE 2.2

World Grain Production

MILLION TONS

WORLD GRAIN PRODUCTION, 1950–91

KILOGRAMS

WORLD GRAIN PRODUCTION PER PERSON, 1950–91

Source: US Department of Agriculture, as presented in L. Brown, C. Flavin, H. Kanes, Vital Signs, 1992: The Trends That Are Shaping Our Future. *New York: W. W. Norton, 1992.*

Ecosystem Resources

The ecology of the earth's biosphere is under tremendous stress. Overconsumption, environmental pollution, land and forest erosion, weather changes, and toxic wastes have degraded many ecosystems. At current rates of consumption we will run out of world oil and copper reserves in about 40 years. Nickel reserves will run out in 66 years. With population doubling in 35 years, these vital resources could be exhausted much faster.

There are 3 to 4.5 million living species on earth. We have detailed knowledge about less than 2 percent of plant species, and less than 1 percent of all other species. Each year up to 10,000 species disappear because humans encroach on their habitats. This unprecedented rate of loss is causing an irreversible decline in biological diversity. We are not even sure of what we are losing, nor do we understand what this loss may mean for the well-being of the planet. (See Figure 2.3.)

Sustainable development implies protecting the diversity and richness of natural resources. It implies conserving non-renewable natural resources, such as fossil fuels, rain forests, and marine ecosystems. (See Figure 2.4.) Economic development that consumes these resources must be paced so that natural ecologies can regenerate themselves. And preserving ecosystems requires special attention to species that are on the verge of extinction.

Consumers are the end users of all natural resources. To avoid resource depletion they need to reassess their consumption habits. However, corporations, as the main intermediaries that grow, harvest, trade, process, and distribute natural resources, can play an important role in resource conservation. The long-term survival of many industries, including agriculture, metals and mining, forest products, and oil depends on the sustained availability of natural resources. Corporations thus have a special responsibility for protecting these resources. They are also better equipped than governments and communities to do so, with the money and information needed for environmental protection. They must help stop irresponsible exploitation of natural resources.

FIGURE 2.3

Deforestation and Decline in Biodiversity

Country	Share of World's Land Area	Share of World's Flowering Species[1]	Annual Deforestation Rate[2]	
	(percent)	(percent)	(square kilometers)	(percent)
Brazil	6.3	22	13,820[3]	0.4
Colombia	0.8	18	6,000	1.3
China	7.0	11	NA	NA
Mexico	1.4	10	7,000	1.5
Australia	5.7	9	NA	NA
Indonesia	1.4	8	10,000	0.9
Peru	1.0	8	2,700	0.4
Malaysia	0.2	6	3,100	1.5
Ecuador	0.2	6	3,400	2.4
India	2.2	6	10,000	2.7
Zaire	1.7	4	4,000	0.4
Madagascar	0.4	4	1,500	1.5

[1]Based on total of 250,000 known species; because of overlap between countries, figures cannot be added. [2]Closed forests only. [3]1990 figure.

Species Type	Observation
Amphibians	Worldwide decline observed in recent years. Wetland drainage and invading species have extinguished nearly half New Zealand's unique frog fauna. Biologists cite European demand for frogs' legs as a cause of the rapid nationwide decline of India's two most common bullfrogs.
Birds	Three-fourths of the world's bird species are declining in population or are threatened with extinction.
Fish	One-third of North America's freshwater fish stocks are rare, threatened, or endangered; one-third of U.S. coastal fish have declined in population since 1975. Introduction of the Nile perch has helped drive half the 400 species of Lake Victoria, Africa's largest lake, to or near extinction.
Invertebrates	On the order of 100 species lost to deforestation each day. Western Germany reports one-fourth of its 40,000 known invertebrates to be threatened. Roughly half the freshwater snails of the southeastern United States are extinct or nearly so.
Mammals	Almost half of Australia's surviving mammals are threatened with extinction. France, Western Germany, the Netherlands, and Portugal all report more than 40 percent of their mammals as threatened.
Carnivores	Virtually all species of wild cats and most bears are declining.
Primates	More than two-thirds of the world's 150 species are endangered.
Reptiles	Of the world's 270 turtle species, 42 percent are rare or endangered.

Source: Worldwatch Institute, Brown, L., et al., State of the World 1992. New York: W. W. Norton, 1992.

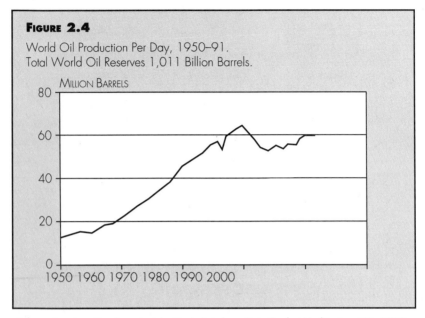

FIGURE 2.4

World Oil Production Per Day, 1950–91.
Total World Oil Reserves 1,011 Billion Barrels.

Source: American Petroleum Institute, Basic Petroleum Data Book. Washington, DC, 1992. 1991 figure is Worldwatch Institute estimate based on British Petroleum, BP Statistical Review of World Energy, London, 1992.

Sustainable Economy and Energy

The core of development activity lies in the economic sector. Economic production influences the environment in many ways. It consumes energy that comes from natural resources. It is a source of environmental pollution and toxic wastes. Carbon emissions from burning fossil fuels have increased fourfold in the last 50 years. (See Figure 2.5.) Industrial transportation and storage are sources of accidental losses of hazardous materials. Urbanization usually accompanies industrialization, and stresses the ecology of specific geographical areas.

A key ingredient of sustainable development is reducing the rate of world energy consumption, and finding a better mix of energy sources. The current level of dependence on fossil fuels that provide most of the world's energy cannot continue. Nor can nuclear energy serve as a substitute—we do not have satis-

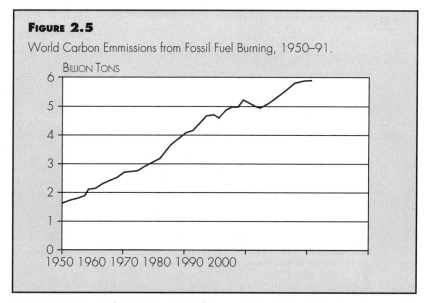

Source: L. Brown, C. Flavin, H. Kanes, *Vital Signs, 1992: The Trends That Are Shaping Our Future. New York: W. W. Norton, 1992.*

factory methods for disposing of radioactive nuclear wastes, which have accumulated exponentially. (See Figure 2.6.)

The per capita energy consumption of industrialized countries is 30 to 80 times that of developing countries. Economic and industrial development of poorer nations would require generation of two to five times the current world levels of energy consumption. The global ecosystem would not be able to withstand such increases in energy generation, particularly from fossil fuels.

Sustainable industrial production requires minimizing the negative influences of production systems on the environment. This means reducing pollution and minimizing toxic and solid wastes. It means increasing production efficiency and reducing technological hazards. It means conserving energy and recycling and reusing materials.

Urbanization that accompanies industrial development has also reached unsustainable proportions. Large cities, such as

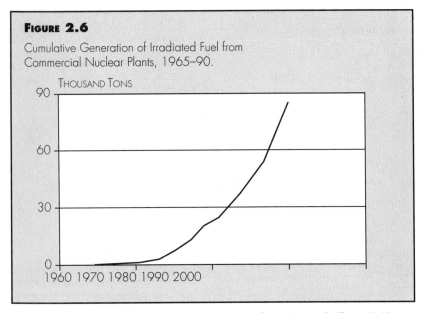

FIGURE 2.6

Cumulative Generation of Irradiated Fuel from
Commercial Nuclear Plants, 1965–90.

Source: Worldwatch, Pacific Northwest Lab, as presented in L. Brown, C. Flavin, H. Kanes,
Vital Signs, 1992: The Trends That Are Shaping Our Future. New York: W. W. Norton,
1992.

Mexico City, Bombay, Calcutta, Lagos, and Caracas, have 30 to
90 percent of their populations living in slums. They lack hygienic living conditions and clean drinking water. Air pollution
and the proximity of populations to hazardous facilities create
exceptional health hazards and technological risks. In industrialized countries in general, the large cities face severe air pollution, congestion, and decaying infrastructure.

Limits of Sustainable Development

The idea of sustainable development is not without shortcomings. Many people have criticized it from different angles. It is
Western-centric in that it uncritically accepts Western definitions
of development and progress. It seeks global management of
ecological resources and systems. Tying global ecological problems together limits the development options of poorer nations

and indigenous peoples. It increases the dependency of developing countries on industrialized countries.

Others have also argued that sustainable development contradicts the logic of capitalism. Capitalism requires the continuous accumulation of capital, through continuous economic growth and consumption. Limiting growth forces capitalist economies into politically and socially unacceptable recessions and depressions.

Moreover, the capitalist mode of production allows producers to externalize the costs of environmental degradation to governments. Since most governments run annual budget deficits, they do not have the necessary financial resources to deal with environmental problems. Governments also lack the knowledge required to remedy environmental problems effectively.

If capitalism is indifferent to ecology, communism is worse. Experiences in the former Soviet Union attest to this. The ecological damage in these countries is several times worse than in industrial Western countries. The culprit is not the ideological system of capitalism or communism. It is the practice of industrialism, which encourages ecologically insensitive technological expansion, resource- and energy-intensive industries, and the unrestrained growth of cities.

Corporations operating in fiercely competitive environments face enormous pressures to cut costs. This limits their ability to spend on safety, environmental protection, health, and maintenance. Managers have high job mobility, short job tenures (three years, on the average), and performance evaluation and compensation oriented to the short term. Therefore, they have little motivation to consider long-term environmental issues in making decisions. Yet corporations are the key engines of economic development. They are also the vehicles on which sustainable development must ride. Sustainable development will succeed or fail depending on our ability to create sustainable corporations.

By emphasizing the role of corporations, I do not mean to downplay the importance of other agents in society. Governments, consumers, communities, and the media have vital roles in sustainable development. Corporate initiatives work within the context of government regulations and policies of population control, urbanization and industrialization. Corporate efforts must also mesh with responsible consumption and mass environmental education. The media can thus play an important role in bringing environmental information to the public.

WHAT IS A SUSTAINABLE CORPORATION?

In the context of sustainable development, what does it mean to be a sustainable corporation? Corporations are groups of individuals with common vision and purpose. They use energy and natural resources as inputs and technological systems of production to convert these inputs into products. Outputs take the form of products and wastes. Corporations seek to meet the multiple and conflicting goals of profitability, growth, competitiveness, and stakeholder demands. Corporate economic and ecological performance depend on resolving conflicts and balancing competing demands. (See Figure 2.7.)

All the key elements of corporations—vision, inputs, throughputs, and outputs (VITO)—have direct consequences for the natural environment. Corporate vision defines the relationship of the company to its natural and human environments. The use of resources and energy depletes natural resources, particularly nonrenewable ones. The system of production affects the natural environment by its emissions and hazards. Managing each corporate element in an ecologically conscious manner can help rather than hinder the pursuit of corporate objectives.

Table 2.1 provides a listing of organizational elements and their components (left-hand column). The center column lists the environmental concerns associated with each element. The right-hand column lists the potential for restructuring each element to improve profitability and gain competitive advantage.

Creating sustainable corporations requires addressing all VITO elements to minimize the environmental and health conse-

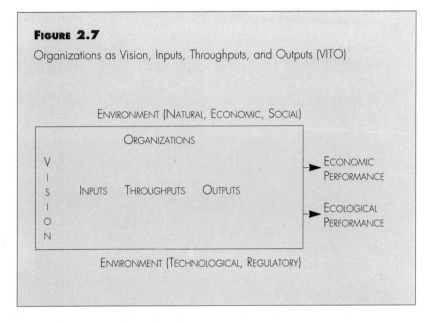

FIGURE 2.7

Organizations as Vision, Inputs, Throughputs, and Outputs (VITO)

quences of corporate activities. This must begin with reassessing and revising the corporate vision. Vision defines corporate self-identity, its relationships with its members, external stakeholders, and nature. In most traditional companies, the corporate vision promotes the welfare of the corporation itself, and ignores nature. These companies view themselves primarily as economic and technological entities. They have little or no conception of their ecological role. Their primary stakeholders are investors and top managers.

There is great potential for changing this traditional vision to support genuine ecological sustainability. A more ecocentric corporate vision would see the firm not only as an economic entity but also an ecological and social entity. It would treat nature as an important stakeholder. It would treat its employees not simply as labor, but as complete persons.

On the input side, there is great potential for restructuring to gain profitability and competitive advantage. Through energy conservation, improved product stewardship, and sustainable harvesting of resources, companies can cut costs and improve their competitive position.

TABLE 2.1

Corporate Environmental Concerns and Potential

CORPORATE ELEMENTS	ENVIRONMENTAL CONCERNS	POSITIVE POTENTIAL
VISION		
Self-identity	Anthropocentrism	Ecocentrism
	Economic/technological enterprise	Social, ecological enterprise
Relationship to members	Members as labor	Concern for the whole person
Relationships with stakeholders	Investors are primary stakeholders	Multiple stakeholders plus nature
Relationships with nature	Nature viewed as resource to be exploited	Nature as a renewable resource
INPUTS		
Raw materials	Depletion of resources	Conservation
	Harm caused by toxic materials	Resource renewal
		User education
Fuels	Fossil fuel depletion	Conservation
		Efficiency
THROUGHPUTS		
Plant	Plant safety/accidents	Preventive maintenance
	Risks to neighborhoods	Liability insurance
	Hazardous materials storage	Eliminate bulk storage
Workers	Occupational hazards Injuries/ill health	Training in humane policies
Wastes	Toxicity, disposal	Reduce, reuse, recycle
	Pollution emissions	Eliminate
Transportation	Spills and losses	Preventive measures
OUTPUTS		
Products	Product safety	Safer designs
	Health consequences	Product improvement
		User education
	Product liability	Insurance
	Environmental impacts	Opportunities for environmentally friendly products
Packaging	Garbage	Recycle, reuse
	Reliability	Design improvements
	Pollution	Pollution control efficiency

During throughput, companies can reduce costs by using cleaner production technologies with closed-loop systems and reduce resource consumption by recycling and reusing wastes. They can provide safe and healthy working conditions within plants and cooperate with communities to reduce risks of accidents. They can adopt more efficient transportation systems. With these actions, companies can improve ecological performance, reduce costs, minimize liabilities and risk exposure, and improve their corporate image.

The opportunity for corporations to minimize product hazards, hazardous wastes, and pollution connected with product output is immense. Companies can address these environmental concerns and are doing so by developing safer and environmentally friendly product and package designs, and engaging in customer education for safe product use and recycling.

Corporations have many influences on the environment. At each point of influence they can improve performance and save money in ways that are good both for the environment and for business. Such win-win solutions are feasible. The box on page 40 shows some nontraditional ways by which companies can foster sustainable development.

A Business Charter for Sustainable Development

To become ecologically sustainable, companies must begin with some acceptable principles for sustainability. In April 1991, 700 industrialists met at the Second World Industry Conference on Environmental Management. They adopted a set of 16 principles (see below) as guidelines for creating sustainable corporations. Since then, top managements of several hundred companies, government organizations, and industry associations have endorsed these principles.

1. *Corporate priority:* To recognize environmental management as among the highest corporate priorities and as a key determinant to sustainable development; to establish policies, programs, and practices for conducting operations in an environmentally sustainable manner.

2. *Integrated management:* To integrate these policies, programs, and practices fully into each business as an essential element of management in all its functions.

3. *Process of improvement:* To continue to improve corporate policies, programs, and environmental performance, taking into account technological developments, scientific understanding, consumer needs, and community expectations, with legal regulations as a starting point; and to apply the same environmental criteria internationally.

4. *Employee education:* To educate, train, and motivate employees to conduct their activities in an environmentally responsible manner.

5. *Prior assessment:* To assess environmental impacts before starting a new activity or project and before decommissioning a facility or leaving a site.

6. *Products and services:* To develop and provide products or services that have no undue environmental impacts and are safe in their intended use, that are efficient in their consumption of energy and natural resources, and that can be recycled, reused, or disposed of safely.

7. *Customer advice:* To advise, and where relevant educate customers, distributors, and the public in the safe use, transportation, storage, and disposal of products provided; and to apply similar considerations to the provision of services.

8. *Facilities and operations:* To develop, design, and operate facilities and conduct activities, taking into consideration the efficient use of energy and materials, the sustainable use of renewable resources, the minimization of adverse environmental impact and waste generation, and the safe and responsible disposal of residual waste.

9. *Research:* To conduct or support research on the environmental impacts of raw materials, products, processes, emissions, and wastes associated with the enterprise and on the means of minimizing such adverse impacts.

10. *Precautionary approach:* To modify the manufacture, marketing, or use of products or services or the conduct of activities, consistent with scientific and technical under-

standing, to prevent serious and irreversible environmental degradation.

11. *Contractors and suppliers:* To promote the adoption of these principles by contractors acting on behalf of the enterprise, encouraging and where appropriate requiring improvements in their practices to make them consistent with those of the enterprise; and to encourage wider adoption of these principles by suppliers.

12. *Emergency preparedness:* To develop and maintain, where significant hazards exist, emergency preparedness plans in conjunction with the emergency services, relevant authorities, and the local community, recognizing potential boundary impacts.

13. *Transfer of technology:* To contribute to the transfer of environmentally sound technology and management methods throughout the industrial and public sectors.

14. *Contributing to the common effort:* To contribute to the development of public policy and to business, government, and inter-governmental programs and educational initiatives that will enhance environmental awareness and protection.

15. *Openness to concerns:* To foster openness and dialogue with employees and the public, anticipating and responding to their concerns about the potential hazards and impacts of operations, products, wastes, or services, including those of trans-boundary or global significance.

16. *Compliance and reporting:* To measure environmental performance; to conduct regular environmental audits and assessments of compliance with company requirements, legal requirements, and these principles; and periodically to provide appropriate information to the board of directors, shareholders, employees, the authorities, and the public.

This charter contains many excellent but general ideas to create sustainable corporations. It places a higher priority on environmental issues than is currently accorded to them. But from

HOW TO PROMOTE SUSTAINABLE DEVELOPMENT IN YOUR COMPANY

1. Expand your primary mission from economic performance to ecological performance. Aim at becoming an ecologically sustainable corporation.

2. Introduce a comprehensive environmental management program. Create ecologically responsible strategies, products, production systems, and waste-management practices.

3. Get involved in solving problems of global sustainable development, including food security, ecosystem protection, reducing population, and conserving energy and resources.

4. Establish a focus on developing countries, which need the greatest help in sustainable development. Transfer environmentally sound technologies to developing countries.

5. Seek ways of addressing local ecological and socio-economic problems in developing countries. Help local communities to practice ecologically sound economic development. This may involve choosing labor-intensive production systems to expand employment. It may require choosing product and packaging designs and waste-management practices suitable to local ecological conditions.

6. Engage government policymakers in creating regulations and infrastructures that encourage sustainable development.

7. Cooperate with ecologically and socially oriented non-governmental organizations to increase community awareness of ecological problems. Develop partnerships with these NGOs for solving these problems.

a radical environmental perspective, the charter still falls short of needed changes.

Radical environmentalists fault the charter for being reformist in character, and not radical enough. It allows companies to continue doing what they are doing, with some incremental environmental modifications. It does not question the complete process of industrial development. It does not ask corporations to assess their business portfolios and activities. It does not suggest abandoning products and technologies that cannot be remedied in the short term.

Despite its shortcomings, the charter has much to offer corporations seriously interested in becoming environmentally sustainable. The challenge facing business is to convert the rhetoric of this charter into reality. This can be done by putting resources into the sustainable policies and programs alluded to in the charter. For this, industry needs to establish an action agenda in four areas:

1. It must promote open dialogue and education among employees, communities in which companies operate, and the public.
2. Companies must aggressively conserve energy, and control waste and emissions from production. They must make public commitments to reduce and manage wastes and emissions by setting measurable goals. They must measure their progress toward those goals and share this information publicly.
3. Companies must accept responsibility for the effects of their materials and products on the environment, from inception to disposal.

Finally, the global economy requires sustainable corporations to tailor their products to the needs and environmental exigencies of local markets. They can no longer simply sell standard products developed for one market in the rest of the world. A product or package that is environmentally sound in one country may be unacceptable in another. Nor can companies sell banned hazardous products in foreign countries, simply because these countries lack protective regulations. Many leading companies are pursuing a variety of environmental efforts to implement these ideas. (See Table 2.2.)

Clearly, survival of life on the planet as we know it depends in large part on how corporations respond to environmental challenges. If they continue along the environmentally exploitative paths of the past, soon there will not be much left to exploit. The power of the idea of ecological sustainability lies in the opportunities it opens up. It does not resist growth per se. It challenges us to look for ecologically sound forms of economic development. Environmentally sustainable economic growth is not only a possibility, it is the only viable option we have.

TABLE 2.2

Companywide Pollution-Prevention Programs and Goals*

COMPANY AND PROGRAM	SCOPE	GOAL	ACCOMPLISHMENTS
Allied Signal waste-reduction program	Includes waste minimization under RCRA, as nonhazardous waste, and evaluates various disposal alternatives and methods for detoxification Plant and project basis	Reduce the quantity and toxicity of hazardous waste that must be stored, treated, or disposed of as economically practicable	The amount of cyclohexylamine waste produced in 1987 was only 15% of the volume of the same waste produced in 1984 The amount of waste finish oil was reduced nearly 90% from 1984 to 1987
Amoco waste-minimization program (1983)	Primary focus on minimizing hazardous-waste disposal, also minimize and track nonhazardous wastes	Eliminate the generation and disposal of hazardous wastes	Between 1983 and 1988, Amoco reduced its hazardous waste by 86%, saving the company about $50 million
AT&T environmental program	Industrial source reduction and toxic chemical use substitution are priorities	Achieve a 50% reduction of CFCs by 1991, and 100% by 1994. Eliminate toxic air emissions of all types by the year 2000, with a 50% reduction by 1993 and a 95% reduction by 1995 Decrease disposal of total manufacturing process wastes by 25% by 1994	Using a BIOACT solvent derived from citrus fruits and other organic compounds to clean electronic equipment. Eliminated CFC use in circuitboard manufacturing process through use of the AT&T low solid fluxer

continued

TABLE 2.2 CONTINUED

Companywide Pollution-Prevention Programs and Goals*

COMPANY AND PROGRAM	SCOPE	GOAL	ACCOMPLISHMENTS
Boeing waste-minimization program	Focus is on process changes which reduce the volume and/or toxicity of hazardous materials used in operations	Reduce use of hazardous materials Minimize the generation of hazardous waste Ensure proper handling and disposal of all wastes	Case study: a chemical substitution in one photoresist stripping operation has increased stripping speeds by 50% and, because of its longer useful life, should reduce annual hazardous waste generation by 50%
Chevron save money and reduce toxics program (SMART, 1987)	SMART adopts EPA's hierarchy, with an emphasis on industrial source reduction, toxic chemical use substitution, and recycling for hazardous and nonhazardous solid wastes	Reduce hazardous waste generation by 65% by 1992 and recycle what is left Find nontoxic alternatives to toxic materials and processes Devise safer operating procedures to reduce accidental releases Ensure that pollution reductions in one area don't transfer pollution to another	From 1987 to 1990, Chevron reduced hazardous waste by 60% and saved more than $10 million in disposal costs Case study: Chevron used to dispose of tank bottoms in landfills. It now uses a centrifuge to separate oil from water, leaving only a small amount of solid to be landfilled (less than 5% of the original sludge)

TABLE 2.2 *CONTINUED*

Companywide Pollution-Prevention Programs and Goals*

COMPANY AND PROGRAM	SCOPE	GOAL	ACCOMPLISHMENTS
Dow waste reduction always pays (WRAP, 1986)	Industrial source reduction and on-site recycling	Increase management support for waste-reduction activities, establish a recognition and reward system for individual plants, compile waste-reduction data, and communicate information on waste-reduction activities Decrease SARA 313 air emissions by 50% by 1995, when compared with 1988 Decrease toxic air emissions (lb/year) 71% by December 1992 (base year December 1988)	SARA 313 overall releases are down from 12,252 tons in 1987 to 9,659 tons in 1989, a 21% reduction. Off-site transfers are down from 2,855 tons in 1987 to 2,422 tons in 1989, a reduction of 15%. Air emissions for 1989 showed a 54% decrease from 1984
General Dynamics zero discharge (1985)	Industrial source reduction, toxic chemical use substitution, recycling, treatment, and incineration	Have no RCRA manifested wastes leaving company facilities	Nearly 40 million lb of hazardous-waste discharge eliminated from 1984 to 1988 (approx. 72%), while sales increased from $7.3 billion to $9.35 billion over same period

continued

TABLE 2.2 *CONTINUED*

Companywide Pollution-Prevention Programs and Goals*

COMPANY AND PROGRAM	SCOPE	GOAL	ACCOMPLISHMENTS
General Electric pollution, waste, and emissions reduction program (POWER, 1989)	Program encompasses all waste streams (e.g., hazardous, nonhazardous, packaging, and ultimate disposal of product) and adopts EPA's hierarchy which places source reduction first	Prevent or minimize "the generation or release of wastes and pollutants, to the extent technically feasible, throughout the life cycle of the product, including its design, production, packaging and ultimate fate in the environment" Decrease toxic air emissions (lb/year) by 90% by December 1993 (base year December 1988	GE Appliances' Louisville plant has reduced its production of hazardous wastewater-treatment sludge by 95%; GE Plastics' Ottawa plant has reduced its butadiene emissions by more than 90%; GE Medical Systems' E. Dale Trout plant has reduced its generation of hazardous waste by 74%; businesswide, GE Power Delivery has reduced its CFC usage by 72%; and, companywide, GE has reduced its SARA 313 reported releases by 11% from 1987 to 1988
Goodyear toxic air emissions reduction	Industrial source reduction	Decrease toxic air emissions (lb/year) by 71% by January 1991 (base year December 1988)	Decreased air emissions from operations through improved maintenance and monitoring of equipment and through decreased use of acrylonitrile, butadiene, and styrene

TABLE 2.2 *CONTINUED*

Companywide Pollution-Prevention Programs and Goals*

COMPANY AND PROGRAM	SCOPE	GOAL	ACCOMPLISHMENTS
IBM	Industrial source reduction and toxic chemical use substitution are priorities, followed by re-cycling, reuse, and reclamation, incineration, detoxification, and disposal in a secure or sanitary landfill, in that order	Pledged to eliminate ozone-depleting chemicals from IBM products and processes by end of 1993 and to recycle 50% of solid waste by 1992	Hazardous waste generation was reduced 38% from 1984 to 1988; 84% of IBM's hazardous waste was recycled; 28% of all solid waste from IBM U.S. operations was recycled in 1988; IBM U.S. emissions were reduced 20% from 1987 to 1988; and IBM U.S. had a decrease of 25% in its CFC emissions between 1987 and 1988
Monsanto priority one (TRI wastes)	Source reduction, reengineering, process changes, reuse, and recycling to reduce hazardous air emissions and TRI solid, liquid, and hazardous wastes	A 90% reduction in hazardous air emissions from 1987 to 1992 A 70% reduction in TRI solid, liquid, and gaseous wastes from 1987 to 1995	From 1987 to 1990, Monsanto achieved a 39% reduction in hazardous air emissions

continued

TABLE 2.2 *CONTINUED*

Companywide Pollution-Prevention Programs and Goals*

COMPANY AND PROGRAM	SCOPE	GOAL	ACCOMPLISHMENTS
Polaroid toxic use and waste-reduction program (TUWR, 1987	Industrial source reduction and toxic chemical use substitution are priorities, followed by re-cycling and reuse	Reduce toxic use at the source and waste per unit of production by 10% per year in each of the 5 years ending in 1993 and, as a corollary, emphasize increased recycling of waste materials within the company	Using 1988 as the base year, Polaroid's Environmental Accounting and Reporting System (EARS) reported an 11% reduction in toxic use and waste during 1989
Scott Paper	Integrated and multi-faceted approach, including source reduction, recycling and reuse of materials, and landfilling of unusable residual waste	Design products and packaging to reduce volume of waste material, which Scott terms "source reduction" Decrease dioxin levels at paper mills by reducing chlorine usage or altering its method of application, or by adopting new technologies or replacements for chlorine bleaching	By the end of 1989, about 20% of the pulp used for sanitary tissue products was made from recycled fiber, and Scott plans to approxi-mately double its recycled capacity The Duffel, Belgium, mill uses a process that uses less water and less fiber Developed a system for source reduction known as "precycling" in which paper products are packaged in larger quantities, thus saving materials which would other-wise have been wasted

TABLE 2.2 *CONTINUED*

Companywide Pollution-Prevention Programs and Goals*

COMPANY AND PROGRAM	SCOPE	GOAL	ACCOMPLISHMENTS
Xerox	Toxic chemical use substitution, materials recovery, and recycling	Reduce hazardous waste generation by 50% from 1990 to 1995	Substituting d-limonene for chlorinated solvents allowed Xerox to reduce the amount of solvents emitted to the atmosphere from about 200,000 lb in 1982 to an estimated 17,000 lb in 1990 A high-pressure water strip operation has enabled Xerox to recycle 800,000 lb nickel and 2 million lb of aluminum tubes per year, and to return 160,000 lb of selenium to suppliers for reuse

*A number of companies were reviewed but not included in this table because their pollution-prevention programs have not been expressed in terms of quantifiable goals or accomplishments.

Source: "Pollution Prevention 1991, Progress on Reducing Industrial Pollutants," U.S. EPA, October 1991, EPA-21P-3003; and Kolluru, 1993.

*L*isten to these voices. They are not the chief druids of the environmental movement. They are corporate leaders exhorting corporations to take environmental issues seriously. They see environmental responsiveness as an integral part of business decision-making and as something that will restructure business and society in the coming decade. They see it as a business imperative.

Corporations that fulfill this imperative will be able to gain competitive advantage; attract and keep customers; reduce exposure to technological risk and liability; minimize regulatory actions against them; satisfy multiple stakeholders; and gain legitimacy. Greening is thus good business policy.

This chapter looks at the business benefits of greening. It shows that greening can help companies in total quality management, in gaining competitive advantage and in entering global markets.

TOTAL QUALITY MANAGEMENT

Total quality management is at center stage in the business world, led by the Japanese. Today, in many industries, Japanese companies have been able to outsell their competitors worldwide because of quality. Their success has prompted a broad-based movement in total quality management in the United States and around the world.

Total quality management is a way of thinking and a set of management techniques. Its primary objective is quality, not profits. It assesses product and production process quality and seeks continuous improvements in them. It promotes the values and attitudes of quality enhancement. It considers customers, suppliers, and other business associates as partners in quality improvement.

The values underlying quality management and environmental management are mutually reinforcing, so they can be

Global Environmental Competitiveness

Make environmental considerations and concerns part of any decision you make, right from the beginning. Don't think of it as something extra you throw in the pot.

RICHARD CLARKE, CEO, PACIFIC GAS & ELECTRIC

Avoiding environmental incidents remains the single greatest imperative facing industry today.

EDGAR WOOLARD, CEO, DUPONT

Environmentalism will be the next major political idea, just as conservatism and liberalism have been in the past.

EDITH WEINER, PARTNER,
WEINTER, EDRICH & BROWN, CONSULTANTS

The 1990s will be the decade of the environment.

PRESIDENT, PETROLEUM MARKETERS ASSOCIATION

combined to support each other. This compatibility resolves a vexing problem of corporate environmentalism—getting workers to believe in it. But employees convinced about one can easily be convinced about the other.

Some companies combine quality management with environmental management to create total quality environmental management (TQEM). TQEM encourages auditing corporate environmental and safety performance periodically to assess its status. It focuses on improving quality of the work environment and the broader natural environment, emphasizing pollution prevention, waste reduction, and getting things done right the first time (versus cleaning up afterwards).

Procter & Gamble has built its entire environment, energy, and safety program on the idea of TQEM. Through membership in Global Environmental Management Initiative (GEMI), companies such as AT&T, Amoco, Browning Ferris, Boeing, Procter & Gamble, and Johnson and Johnson are improving both environmental and quality performance. GEMI has successfully created unified quality/environment strategies and promotes a "worldwide business ethic for environmental management and sustainable development."

IBM's Manassas, Virginia, semiconductor plant uses TQEM to deal with regulatory reporting. There are 15,000 pages of state and federal environmental regulations covering the company's activities. The company assigns to individuals and groups the responsibility for implementing each regulation. It monitors progress on implementation. It analyzes reports using quality management techniques and enhances the efficiency of regulatory reporting using a computerized data base. As a result, the plant was able to speed up filing of regulatory reports.

Florida Power and Light Company made dramatic gains in environmental management, using the quality management techniques of cause-and-effect fishbone diagrams and Pareto charts to identify the main shortcomings in its environmental programs. One was employees' lack of understanding of hazardous-

GLOBAL ENVIRONMENTAL MANAGEMENT INITIATIVE (GEMI)

This Washington, DC-based organization is a cooperative effort of the member companies listed below. Its objective is to promote the implementation of the *Business Charter for Sustainable Development* (quoted in Chapter 2) developed by the International Chamber of Commerce. It has designed an environmental self-assessment program to aid companies in quantifying and tracking their progress on the 16 principles of the charter. It conducts conferences and workshops for corporate managers to share best environmental management practices.

GEMI Members

Allied-Signal • Amoco Corporation • AT&T
The Boeing Company • Browning-Ferris Industries
Digital Equipment Corporation • The Dow Chemical
Company Duke Power Company • Eastman Kodak
Dupont Florida Power and Light • ICI Americas
Merck & Co. • Occidental Petroleum
Procter & Gamble • The Southern Company • Tenneco
Union Carbide Corporation • USX Corporation
W. R. Grace & Co.

waste-handling processes, so the company initiated annual environmental training of employees, and changed waste-handling procedures and labeling programs. By doing this, it reduced the number of annual citations for environmental violations from 32 in 1985, to 21 in 1986, to two in 1990.

In 1985, Dupont decided to cut its manufacturing waste 35 percent by technical means. This strategy turned out to be very time-consuming. So, in 1987, it added waste reduction to the agenda of the company's quality management teams. They applied the systematic analysis of quality management to the company's waste problems, leading to dramatic gains. One Dupont plastics plant saved 15 million pounds of plastic waste a year by making only modest changes in production and shipping procedures.

American companies are now implementing quality management widely. Environmental programs can easily piggyback on them. The benefits of quality management also stand to gain. Improving the quality of the work environment and making working conditions safe contribute to worker satisfaction and to better product and process quality. Similarly, improving the natural environment increases community and customer satisfaction. This strengthens community and customer support for businesses.

GREEN COMPETITIVE ADVANTAGE

The second business reason for greening corporations is competitive advantage. There are many sources of competitive advantage for companies—low cost, product differentiation, and satisfying market-niche demands are some. Each of these sources of competitive advantage can be given an environmental twist.

3M's "Pollution Prevention Pays" program illustrates the potential for cutting costs through environmental programs. In its first 15 years—1975 to 1989—this program established 2,511 pollution prevention projects and cut pollution per unit of production by half. It prevented discharge of more than 500,000 tons of pollutants and saved the company $500 million.

Product differentiation strategies can use greening. Loblaw International Merchants, Procter & Gamble, and The Limited are differentiating their products for environmentally conscious customers. Other companies such as The Body Shop and Seventh Generation sell *only* green products, focusing on niches of environmentally sensitive customers in their industries. Still other companies are producing pollution control equipment, such as gas scrubbers, air filters, waste incinerators, sewage treatment plants, and bioremediation systems.

Private-sector expenditures on environmental protection equipment in the United States now exceed $50 billion a year. The global demand for environmentally friendly products is more than $200 billion a year, and growing exponentially. Such demands and opportunities have encouraged companies to make fundamental product and packaging changes to remain competitive.

For example, by replacing ozone-depleting chlorofluorocarbons (CFCs) with safer alternatives, Dupont has maintained its competitive leadership in this industry segment. The Body Shop has gained competitive edge over giant cosmetic companies such as Unilever, Procter & Gamble, and Revlon by pioneering an "all natural" line of cosmetics and body care products. In 1991, McDonald's abandoned Styrofoam clamshell hamburger packaging in response to consumer demands and to overcome Burger King's paper packaging.

Five years ago the green consumer segment was a tiny market niche. Today it is becoming a mainstream trend in many consumer-goods industries. Customers are demanding green products and packaging more friendly to the environment. Some consumers are willing to pay higher prices for environmentally sound products, and they are seeking more information about contents, use, disposal, and recyclability. As a result, hundreds of new and reformulated green products are now on the market, along with dozens of green consumer guides to evaluate them and organizations like Green Seal and Blue Angel to certify them. Selling green consumer products clearly presents a strategic opportunity.

GLOBAL MARKETS

A third business reason for becoming environmentally responsive lies in the demographics of global markets. A significant part of consumer demand in the future will come from the developing world. Three-fourths of world population currently lives in these countries; by the year 2030, nearly 84 percent of world population will. Many such countries have a significant middle class with sizeable purchasing power—between 300 million and 500 million worldwide.

Multinational companies are eager to penetrate these vast markets. In the past this meant simply transferring existing products and technologies to other countries. But it is no longer ecologically practical to push Western consumerist lifestyles and products on developing countries. Instead, the products, technologies, and production and distribution systems must be compatible with their social aspirations, economic conditions, and ecological resources.

The history of technology transfer to developing countries is full of economic and ecological mistakes. Often the products/technologies were obsolete "sunset" technologies that were being dumped on the developing world. For example, until the mid-1970s, Western computer companies routinely passed off outdated computers to the Third World. Even as late as 1985, they were selling them punch-card computer systems (a 30-year-old technology).

There was little consideration given to environmental influences of transferred technologies. The World Bank and other international financial institutions financed many economic development projects that had disastrous environmental consequences. Companies exported hazardous products banned in the West to developing countries with weak regulations. These products included asbestos, DDT pesticides, untested drugs, and hazardous wastes, along with outdated production facilities.

In 1984, several Western governments signed the Montreal Protocol on ozone depletion. This treaty called for a world-wide phaseout of CFCs by the year 2000. The same year, Western multinational companies were selling CFC technology to developing countries.

Such experiences have made developing countries suspicious. They are now realizing that economic development and technology transfer bring along environmental problems. They are demanding state-of-the-art technologies, which are often more hazardous and complex. Simultaneously, their large and growing populations have caused severe environmental degradation. This puts new burdens of managing technological and environmental risks in foreign environments.

The accident at Union Carbide's pesticide plant in Bhopal, India, is one example. The use of infant formula in developing countries is another. It caused tremendous harm. The formula itself was safe and widely used in industrialized countries. When marketed aggressively in Africa, it caused the deaths and malnutrition of millions of babies. Mothers in these countries used impure water, or diluted it too much to save money, or reused leftover formula. Some users could not read labels and instructions on the packages because they were illiterate.

Multinational companies that hope to succeed in global markets thus will need to develop local institutional capacity to manage the environmental and health risks associated with their technologies. This includes design of environmentally appropriate products and packaging for different local markets. The companies must educate consumers about ecologically safe product use and disposal. They must establish international product stewardship and global standards for pollution control, industrial safety, and environmental management. And they need to develop new environmental impact assessment techniques for foreign environments, and incorporate environmental and health costs into their business calculations.

The payoffs of developing this sensitivity can be enormous. Companies that show concern for environmental and health issues will have a special competitive edge in developing world markets. Merck & Co., Inc., provides an example of how such concerns can translate into business opportunity. Being a pharmaceutical company, it has the "human environment" as its main concern.

Over the years Merck has donated many medicines and pharmaceutical technologies to developing countries. It gave the technology for making antibiotics to Japan in 1950. This enabled the Japanese to cope with infectious diseases in the aftermath of World War II. Merck also gave technology for manufacturing antiseptics to China. Now it is donating medicine to cure river blindness to African countries, where this disease is a scourge to millions of people.

Because of these efforts Merck is a global company today. It has strong presence in most developing countries, which are likely to become huge pharmaceutical markets in coming years.

We should not underestimate the economic benefits that follow such benevolent actions. They offer goodwill, good public image, and more. They reflect enlightened self-interest and good citizenship. A company eventually reaps business benefits from these acts. In the short run, it gets modest tax benefits. In the long run, it creates a positive climate and goodwill in foreign countries. This goodwill eases the company's entry into new markets. It creates a positive public image of the company. It makes the company's presence in foreign countries more acceptable, even welcome.

Purely from a business point of view, greening of corporations makes sense. Greening is compatible with quality management and can enable companies to gain competitive advantage. This can help companies enter the huge evolving markets in developing countries.

Environmental efforts do cost money. However, even in environmentally progressive companies, they do not exceed 1 per-

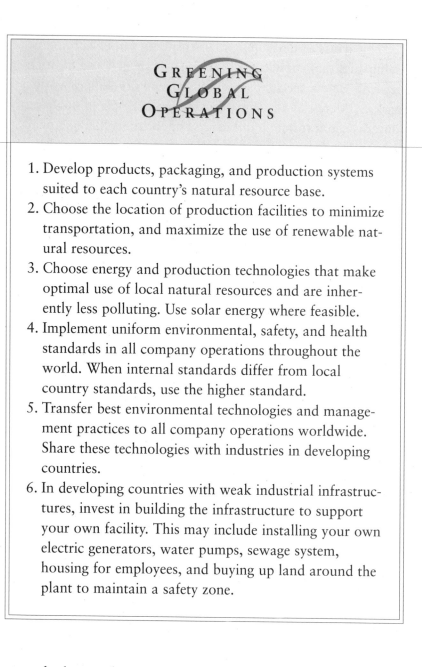

GREENING
GLOBAL
OPERATIONS

1. Develop products, packaging, and production systems suited to each country's natural resource base.
2. Choose the location of production facilities to minimize transportation, and maximize the use of renewable natural resources.
3. Choose energy and production technologies that make optimal use of local natural resources and are inherently less polluting. Use solar energy where feasible.
4. Implement uniform environmental, safety, and health standards in all company operations throughout the world. When internal standards differ from local country standards, use the higher standard.
5. Transfer best environmental technologies and management practices to all company operations worldwide. Share these technologies with industries in developing countries.
6. In developing countries with weak industrial infrastructures, invest in building the infrastructure to support your own facility. This may include installing your own electric generators, water pumps, sewage system, housing for employees, and buying up land around the plant to maintain a safety zone.

cent of sales, on the average. Very often, environmental costs are recoverable. Many companies, such as 3M and Dow Chemical, have made greening financially self-sustaining. In short, if done right, greening can be a good financial investment.

Ethical and
Political Imperatives

Green Eggs and Ham
I do not like it, Uncle Sam,
Do something quick, about this scam
It's all those green products, damn.
One more hype, and I'll upchuck and scram,
I do not like it, Uncle Sam,
I do not like it, Uncle Sam.

Companies are selling green eggs and ham,
They sell "green" wherever they can.
Green detergents, clothing, cars, green Van,
Green mousse for the oily-hairdo man,
Dah'ling, now you can get a 'green' tan.
Natural whole wheat, oatmeal and bran,
The entire country is on a green plan.

I do not like green eggs and ham.
I do not like them Uncle Sam.
I do not believe eggs can be green,
They can be white, off-white, and cream.
But Green? I've never heard of that.
And that too, without cholesterol and fat?

I tell you, I smell a rat.
Would I eat them on a train?
Would I eat them with fried brain?
Would I like them well done?
They tell me "Try them, they are such fun."
Not on a train,
Not with fried brain,
Not well done,
NO, they are not fun.

Green eggs? That's too weird you see.
Green ham? What kind of gourmet would I be?
I will not eat them, not one grain,
I will not eat them, I want to stay sane.

Shouldn't someone regulate green claims,
Stop these nonsensical consumer games.
Stop charlatans accumulating wealth and fame,
Who should unsuspecting consumers blame?
Come and rescue us Uncle Sam,
From advertisers' clatter and clam.
Al Gore promised a balanced earth,
Of promises we have no dearth,
If we are elected, claimed Bill and he,
Ozone protection we guarantee,
Protect rain forests, biodiversity,
Even a Global Warming treaty,
But now where is your action program,
I do not see it Uncle Sam,
I do not like it Uncle Sam.

AN ADAPTATION OF "GREEN EGGS AND HAM,"
WITH APOLOGIES TO DR. SEUSS

*E*thics and morality are relative. They depend on beliefs, values, and customs of individuals, groups, regions, and nations. They vary by race, class, caste, culture, ethnicity, religion, and ideology. Then what case can we make for all corporations to pursue an "environmental ethic"? What is the ethical imperative that faces corporations concerning the environment?

THE ETHICS OF GREENING

Environmental ethics depend on how we understand the relationship of humans to nature and how we implement that understanding through our organizations and institutions. Historically, most world religions have placed humans at the center of this relationship (*anthropocentrism*). This bias views humans as separate from nature, and superior to it. Nature exists for the sake of human welfare. Humans arrogate to themselves an unquestionable right to subdue, use, and exploit nature without regard for any limits. Nature has no right to exist for its own sake.

This view has been particularly true for Christianity, the dominant religion of the industrialized West and the value base of modern capitalism. Lyn White (1967) has persuasively argued that Christianity emphasizes the dominion of nature by man. It preaches an ethic of human relations that subordinates the natural world. It sanctions an exploitative environmental ethic.

In the pre-industrial world this belief had functional value. It gave impetus for humans to protect themselves from natural hazards and survive them. It encouraged them to use natural resources to build communities and establish civilizations.

With the arrival of industrial technologies, humans developed immense power and capacity to exploit nature and consume it. As a result, humans have consumed more natural resources in the last 200 years than in the previous million years. This rapid exploitation is altering the earth's natural equilibrium.

Anthropocentrism is now being questioned within Christianity, and within other major religions, too. A new ecological morality is emerging. A new critical mood is on the rise in world religions, questioning the old human-centered world views and acknowledging the rights and inevitability of nature to exist on its own.

Questioning the old values leads us to new visions of eco-justice. People are beginning to see the unfairness of arrogating all rights to humans, and none to nature. They perceive this as unfair to other species, and not in the best interest of humans. Animal-rights protection groups have highlighted the plight of animals. Cruelty to animals caused by scientific research, fur trapping, wildlife hunting and poaching, and loss of habitats are now moral issues.

Eco-justice is also concerned with social justice for "natural resource communities," communities that derive their subsistence from the natural resources around them. Millions of people (indigenous peoples, tribal people, the rural poor, for example) depend on local natural sources for drinking water and crop irrigation. They get food, medicinal herbs, wood for fuel and shelter materials from local rivers, lakes, forests, and other common resources. Destroying nature destroys their sustenance.

This destruction is done by industrial activities (mining, manufacturing, and mechanized farming) and development projects (dams, roads, and urbanization). Similarly, imposing a market economy on natural resource communities limits their ability to sustain themselves. It forces rural poor to move to crowded urban areas. The gross injustice this creates has led to major conflicts over environmentally harmful development projects.

Even if humans do not respect the rights of nature, it will continue to exist, despite exploitation. However, it may become more hostile to human needs. By recognizing the rights of nature, humans can create powerful laws for protecting nature and preventing a few ruthless people from exploiting its resources, and thereby destroying it for all.

The translation of moral judgments to corporate responsibilities for preservation of nature is a complex issue. Corporations have other social responsibilities. Among other things, they are responsible for earning a reasonable return for investors, creating jobs, ensuring community stability, and providing safe products.

On the surface, some of these social responsibilities may conflict with corporate ecological concerns. Examples are the "Spotted Owl versus logging jobs" in the Pacific Northwest, and the "Snail Darter versus fishing business" in the South. People perceive these situations as conflicts because they are cast in polarizing terms. They position ecological preservation against jobs and business interests.

A narrow view of these conflicts leads to partisan solutions and compromises driven by political considerations. Nature or communities win or lose, depending on the relative political power of environmental groups and industry. The ethical question these conflicts raise is not whether corporations should choose between protecting human interests or ecological ones. Both interests are important and deserve consideration. The central issue here is for corporations to invent a broader socio-ecological ethic.

This broader ethic would apply to all decisions that involve techno-environmental hazards. Decisions would be made on the basis of ecological sustainability, long-term perspective, social participation, transparency, and a longer time frame. Corporate decision processes involving techno-environmental risks should be made as transparent as possible without compromising competitive information. Transparency of decision processes helps in monitoring them, and keeps all parties honest. Extending the time frame of a solution allocates the costs for ecological projects over longer time horizons.

Broad social participation in ecologically sensitive corporate decisions allows more socially acceptable decisions. This participation must be genuine. It must incorporate those groups that will bear the risks of technological decisions. Such participation is encouraged through Technology Assessment programs in Europe, and the right-to-know laws (SARA Title III) in the United States. These are efforts to inform communities and solicit their participation in local technological risk management.

How well corporations fulfill their ecological responsibility will determine their legitimacy. Public support for business enterprise as a whole hinges on fulfilling this responsibility. By greening, corporations can meet their moral obligations, augment their legitimacy, and burnish their public image.

THE GREEN POLITICAL IMPERATIVE

The ethical imperative depends on voluntary acceptance of responsibility by corporations. The political imperative pressures companies to be environmentally responsible. The past decade has witnessed a dramatic rise in political pressure on corporations to address environmental problems.

In the United States alone, there were thousands of environmental regulations enacted at the local, state, and federal levels. Ironically, this was during the conservative Reagan and Bush administrations, which promised "to get the government off the backs of the people." However, improved administrative systems for monitoring and implementing policies did not accompany the increase in regulation.

This rise of regulation can be attributed to the mainstreaming of reform environmentalism. It is no longer a movement at the margin of society; it is now a concern of the middle classes. The middle classes are moving toward voluntary simplicity involving less material consumption, a slower pace, harmonious relations of people to nature, and an orientation to family life. Decentralized, independent environmental movements have emerged to give voice to these values. In addition, globalization of environmental problems has led to widespread sharing of environmental concerns. These factors make environmental politics permanent, ubiquitous, and resilient.

The rise of radical environmentalism has added fuel to the political fire. Elections at all levels increasingly involve environmental issues, linked to the traditionally important issues of the economy, defense, social programs, and foreign policy.

Public concern is both positive and negative. More and more people are involved in community waste recycling programs, use of environment friendly products and services, and energy conservation. On the other hand, the NIMBY ("not in my back yard") phenomenon is changing local politics in fundamental ways. Before Three Mile Island and Love Canal, the public trusted the government and corporations to deal with technological risks, presuming that these institutions had enough technological expertise to protect them. But these events showed that the public was not safe.

Also, corporate and government administrative institutions have progressively become more complex and inaccessible, motivating people to take an active role in local risk decisions. So people started to involve themselves in protecting their communities, instead of relying on governments and corporations. Now communities around the country seek control over technological risks to the environment.

Outside the United States, the green political movement is even more noticeable. In Europe, green parties made significant gains in the past two decades. In Germany, Norway, and Denmark, green parties are now a national force. In these and other countries, major political parties have developed strong environmental platforms. Sometimes these platforms are only of rhetorical and symbolic value. In other cases they are not practical in their goals. Nonetheless, concern for ecology is now a very potent variable in electoral politics here and overseas.

The unification of European markets in 1992 has brought uniform environmental, safety, and health standards to the member countries. The guiding principle for these standards is *prevention* of further environmental degradation. Articles 100A and 130T of the Single European Act define the minimum standards. They are both more stringent and more comprehensive than existing standards, even in nations that are environmental leaders. They also allow individual member states to adopt, voluntarily, standards that are even more stringent.

The November 1989 report by the Community Environment Ministers entitled "1992, The Environmental Dimension," has gone farther. It articulates four new principles that are reshaping environmental policies of member states:

1. Make the polluter pay.
2. Delegate decision-making to the most local level of political authority.
3. Take economic efficiency and cost effectiveness into account.
4. Be legally efficient, that is, use readily enforceable legal instruments.

Environmental sentiment in Japan is also on the rise. Japan is home to some of the worst environmental disasters: the Minamata mercury poisonings and congestion and air pollution in Tokyo are just two examples. And the world environmental community has criticized Japanese industries for drift-net fishing, ruthless cutting of rain forests, and trading in ivory and turtle shells.

However, two factors have slowed environmental progress in Japan. First, powerful business forces have stalled regulation. Second, much of the environmental damage caused by Japanese industrial interests occurs outside Japan: deforestation in Asia and South America, overfishing in international waters, and killing elephants in Africa.

Since the breakdown of Communism, the opening up of the former Soviet Union and its Eastern European satellites has revealed an environmental nightmare. This region suffers tremendous pollution and environmental degradation, especially near industrial sites. These problems are far greater than any encountered in the industrialized West. Former Soviet leader Mikhail Gorbachev was the first to acknowledge environmental problems and the need to deal with them urgently. Since his departure in 1990, and the ensuing economic and political confusion, the environment has again taken a low priority on the political agenda.

However, the environment is now an important element in international relations, and many treaties are concerned with the cross-national aspects of environmental problems. These include the Convention on International Trade in Endangered Species, the 1987 Montreal Treaty on Substances That Deplete the Ozone Layer, the 1988 Protocol on Nitrous Oxide, the 1989 Basel Convention on Control of Transboundary Movements of Hazardous Wastes, and the World Industry Conferences on Environmental Management (WICEM).

The United Nations Conference on Environment Development, held in July 1992 in Rio de Janeiro, Brazil, created the most comprehensive international environmental agreements. These include treaties for controlling global warming, ozone depletion, toxic waste export, deforestation, desertification, food security, and population control. These treaties will lead to establishing new laws, environmental programs, research, and organizations.

The conference also ratified the business environmental charter and put hundreds of new sustainable development programs on the world political agenda. The first environmental conference in 1972 led to the setting up of environmental protection agencies and laws in dozens of countries. Similarly, this conference will further expand national and international commitments to the environment.

There are significant non-market forces in place worldwide, pushing corporations to be ecologically responsible. The environmental movement has now developed strong political and social allies in local cultures. Environmentalism is not likely to disappear. It will be a permanent part of the economic and social landscape of the future.

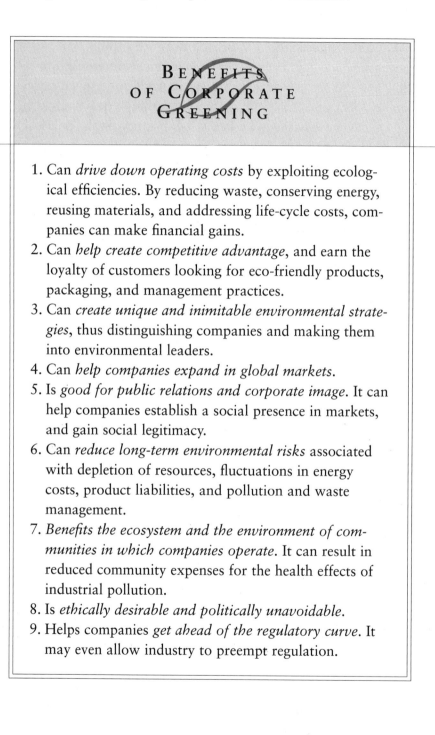

BENEFITS OF CORPORATE GREENING

1. Can *drive down operating costs* by exploiting ecological efficiencies. By reducing waste, conserving energy, reusing materials, and addressing life-cycle costs, companies can make financial gains.
2. Can *help create competitive advantage*, and earn the loyalty of customers looking for eco-friendly products, packaging, and management practices.
3. Can *create unique and inimitable environmental strategies*, thus distinguishing companies and making them into environmental leaders.
4. Can *help companies expand in global markets.*
5. Is *good for public relations and corporate image*. It can help companies establish a social presence in markets, and gain social legitimacy.
6. Can *reduce long-term environmental risks* associated with depletion of resources, fluctuations in energy costs, product liabilities, and pollution and waste management.
7. *Benefits the ecosystem and the environment of communities in which companies operate*. It can result in reduced community expenses for the health effects of industrial pollution.
8. Is *ethically desirable and politically unavoidable.*
9. Helps companies *get ahead of the regulatory curve*. It may even allow industry to preempt regulation.

PART II

WHO IS GREEN: CASE STUDIES OF ENVIRONMENTALLY CORRECT COMPANIES

This part provides examples of companies that have started moving toward ecological sustainability. Each company is at a different stage of achieving this goal, and each has its own approach. The companies were chosen because they are environmental leaders in their respective industries. They have been recognized for such leadership through numerous awards and wide publicity. This choice also tried to create balance in international coverage (North America, Europe, Japan), and in product types (consumer products, durable goods, industrial products). The companies include:

- The Body Shop PLC (UK, personal care products)
- Procter & Gamble, Inc. (USA, consumer products)
- Loblaw International Merchants, Inc. (Canada, groceries retailing)
- Ben and Jerry's Homemade Ice Creams, Inc. (USA, ice cream)
- The Volvo Car Company (Sweden, automobiles)
- The 3M Company (USA, diversified industrial)
- Tokyo Electric Power Company (TEPCO) (Japan, electric utility)

The case studies focus on environmental efforts of each company. The VITO elements introduced in Chapter 2 provide a general framework for the case studies. Each case deals with green vision, inputs, throughputs, and outputs, although not always in that order. This allows the reader to see commonalities as well as differences between the companies.

The cases provide a selective description of environmental programs, an important strength of these companies. This focus on an area of excellence makes the cases somewhat one-sided. This focus is necessary to showcase their ecological orientation, but it does not imply that the companies have no weaknesses. Nor does it mean that they are excellent or socially responsible in all aspects.

Missionary Greening:
The Body Shop

Housewife turned eco-preneur Anita Roddick opened The Body Shop on March 27, 1976, in Brighton, England, to sell all-natural personal care products. By 1991, The Body Shop International PLC was operating in 39 countries, with nearly 600 stores worldwide, 6,000 employees, revenues of £115.6 million, and profits of £20 million. Its revenues, profits, and earnings per share grew at more than 30 percent per year from 1988 through 1990.

For Anita and Gordon Roddick, more important than these financial accomplishments were their social and environmental achievements. Over its lifetime, the company has run 19 major campaigns and completed 475 community projects. These projects focused on causes ranging from protection of rain forests, to elimination of hunger in the Third World, to working with orphans in Romania. Its 1990 petition against animal testing was signed by 2.6 million people. The company recycled 12.5 tons of waste in its UK operations.

The company's insistence on marketing only *environmentally safe natural products* has given it a unique position in the cosmetics industry. Its high level of commitment to environmental policies and programs can be compared to the zeal of a missionary.

This commitment emerges from the ecocentric values of the founders. Both Anita and Gordon Roddick care deeply about environmental issues. Environmental protection and environmental sustainability are part of the mission and vision of the company. The company selects employees, and the employees choose to work for The Body Shop, in large part because of their mutual agreement on environmental values.

This high degree of consistency of environmental values pervades all aspects of the company. It includes product development, production, waste and energy management, consumer protection, and social and environmental policies.

AN ANTI-BUSINESS BUSINESS

The vision driving The Body Shop is best captured in the irreverent pronouncements of Anita Roddick. She starts her autobiography *Body and Soul* with the following admonition:

"I hate the beauty business. It is a monster industry selling unattainable dreams. It cheats. It exploits women. Its major product lines are packaging and garbage. . . .

"To me, the whole notion of a 'beauty' business is profoundly disturbing. What is beauty? I believe beauty is about vivaciousness, and energy and commitment and self-esteem, rather than some ideal arrangement of limbs or facial features as celebrated in fashion magazines and beauty pageants. . . .

"In my view the cosmetics industry should be promoting health and well-being; instead it hypes an outdated notion of glamour and sells false hopes and fantasy. With the muscle of multi-million-dollar advertising budgets, the major cosmetics houses seek to persuade women that they can help them look younger and more 'beautiful.' Yet they know such claims are nonsense.

"What is even worse is that the industry seems to have absolutely no sense of social responsibility; and in its desperate

"If this food has no colourings, no flavourings, no preservatives and no added sugar or salt, then why does it cost more?"

Source: Stan Eales, *Earthtoons*, Wartner Books, copyright 1991. Reprinted with permission from the publisher.

need to chase profits in an area that has been experiencing, at best, sluggish growth for years, it is moving into territory where it should have no place. It is producing lipstick and eye shadow for children in a society where the spread of child pornography is causing increasing concern. It has even launched expensive perfumes for babies and toddlers—how decadent can you get?"

This, coming from the founder and managing director of one of the world's largest cosmetics companies, is baffling. That is, until you realize that Anita Roddick, the housewife turned businesswoman and self-proclaimed loudmouth, is no ordinary woman. She is a visionary of rare talent. Her vision of beauty as *vivaciousness, energy, commitment, and self-esteem* is the basis of a fundamentally different and innovative organizational form. She views business as an engine of social change. The Roddicks have created a company that is primarily an agent of positive social change—while also being financially prosperous.

The company has a highly progressive social conscience, manifested in its many and diverse social and economic development programs. They include preservation of rain forests, fund-raising for Amnesty International, and job training for the homeless in London.

In actualizing its unusual mission, The Body Shop goes against every basic tenet of the cosmetics industry. Its products are all-natural, in an industry dominated by chemical concoctions. The company began with a single store and no financial backing, in an industry full of giant firms. Its shops are franchised. The franchisees own each shop. The Body Shop provides products, advertising, shop designs, and merchandising support. It has never spent a single cent on advertising, in an industry that spends nearly 25 cents of each sales dollar on advertising. The company is loudly outspoken on social and ethical issues facing business, when most other companies maintain a deafening silence about them.

For a company of its size and spread, The Body Shop has a minimal formal structure. It is organized by functions and divisions, but formal administrative structures and allocations of responsibility provide only very general guidance. Responsibility (toward the company, fellow employees, the environment, and society) is part of the company's culture. The employee contract includes an obligation to get involved in community, social, and environmental projects.

The work atmosphere is informal, even casual. Work is loosely structured, collaborative, imaginative, and improvised. In place of the traditional many levels of hierarchy, the company has only a few. The company is working to create a structure with only three levels—department heads, managers, and shop-floor personnel. All new managers and department heads will be interviewed by those who will be working for them.

The difference in wages of the highest and lowest paid employees is modest. The average staff cost (wages plus social security plus pension) in 1991 was £11,600, while the chairman of the company earned £116,000.

THE HIGH MORAL ROAD AS A STRATEGY

The Body Shop does not have a "business strategy" in the conventional sense of the term. It does not identify or create specific product needs, and then design products to fulfill them. It refrains from selling products in as high a volume as possible, with aggressive advertising hype. Instead, its business is based on supplying what is natural and healthful to people who want it. It offers a choice of packaging that allows customers to buy only as much as they need.

The basic strategy is to make business choices on moral grounds. In Anita Roddick's words, "when you take the high moral road it is difficult for anyone to object without sounding like a complete fool." The core idea of her business is fair and honest trading in which both parties benefit: Trading that continually seeks new partners. Trading with traditionally disenfranchised groups, to make them self-supporting. Trade as a moral practice based on Roddick's two basic values of work and love. These values have fostered a strong sense of commitment to and from employees, customers, suppliers, the natural environment, and humanity.

USING NATURAL INGREDIENTS

The Body Shop makes its own products that cleanse, polish, and protect the skin and hair. Every product has only natural ingredients, taken from plants, herbs, fruits, flowers, seeds, nuts, oils, soils, water, and juices. All ingredients come from renewable sources. The Anthropology and Research and Development Department studies skin- and hair-care rituals of other cultures, such as the Kayapo Indians in the Amazon rain forest and the hill tribes of the Humla region in Nepal. Anita Roddick travels to these remote destinations to try out new products and identify local suppliers.

Traditional product recipes are improved upon to increase their safety, durability, stability, and effectiveness. The company uses some preservatives and synthetic fragrances to add variety to its products. At the same time, for ethical reasons, the company does not use certain natural products. It does not use musk, because it is extracted cruelly from the glands of male musk deer. It developed a musk-like perfume from other ingredients. This "White-Musk" is the company's best-selling perfume.

PRODUCT TESTING

Unlike most cosmetics companies, The Body Shop actively opposes and campaigns against animal testing. It believes that animals should not suffer for human vanity. It believes that it is neither right nor necessary nor scientifically accurate to test skin- and hair-care products on animals. It requires suppliers to provide regular, written confirmation that no animal testing took place on their behalf within the previous five years.

The Body Shop chooses ingredients with a long history of safe human use: Nature-based materials such as cocoa butter, lavender oil, chamomile, and kaolin have been used safely for centuries. It has also developed safe and humane alternatives to animal testing. All raw materials are microbiologically tested. For example, Eytex is a natural protein culture test that can predict eye irritation in humans. This test substitutes for the animal-based Draize test. The company is also developing "Testskin"—human skin actually grown in a test tube.

New products are tested by volunteer members of The Body Shop. Volunteers take skin-patch tests at the company's Product Evaluations Clinic. Twenty to 30 volunteers are studied for seven to 24 days. If the product passes in-house tests, it is sent to the University of Wales laboratories for independent testing. Decision to market the product is made only after it passes this independent test.

PRODUCT PACKAGING

The company believes that the main products of the cosmetics industry are packaging and waste. It goes in the opposite direction by eliminating all unnecessary packaging. Each package is designed with three criteria—product compatibility, strength over useful life, and safety. The company encourages customers to refill existing containers by offering a 25-cent discount on each refill.

Customers who do not want to refill packages can return them to The Body Shop for recycling. All plastic bottles have recycling identification. The company uses recycled paper to print all company stationery, brochures, profiles, broadsheets, leaflets, and posters. It shreds all wastepaper at the head office and uses it as padding for mail-order packages. It encourages employees to bring their junk mail, magazines, and telephone directories from home for shredding. It actively campaigns for recycling efforts within communities in which it operates.

PRODUCTION WITH A CONSCIENCE

The Body Shop is primarily a retailing and trading company. It manufactures only a few of the goods it sells. It has a plant in Brighton, England, which mixes ingredients and packages products. These are not heavily polluting or energy intensive operations. Hence the traditional environmental problems associated with manufacturing businesses do not apply.

The Body Shop's energy self-sufficiency policy seeks to minimize energy use and have zero impact on fossil-fuel resources. This policy involves systematic energy audits and conservation programs in its shops, warehouses, plants and transportation, and energy replacement strategies. Its factory in Brighton uses electrical energy supplied by the local utility, which uses fossil fuels to generate it. The company has established wind farms in Scotland to generate electricity which is put back into the utility's electric grid. In the next few years this arrangement will replace all the fossil energy the company consumes with an equivalent amount of wind-generated energy.

Where it does do manufacturing, The Body Shop does so with a social purpose and through the use of simple and small-scale technologies. This simplification is quite appropriate for its soaps, cosmetics, and shampoos, which can be produced economically in small and moderate-size plants. Small-scale plants create limited pollution. This pollution is also easier to eliminate or control.

The use of simple technologies allows the company to use suppliers from poor communities and from developing countries. It encourages economically disadvantaged communities to grow and process ingredients for its products. This provides employment and trade opportunities to these communities.

In 1987, the company refurbished an old factory in Easterhouse, Scotland, to manufacture its own soap. The technology for soap making is simple. It can be implemented with local labor and little infrastructure. At full capacity, this plant will supply about one-third of the company's worldwide sales of soap.

This decision was as much a social decision as a commercial one. It helped develop a community that was economically depressed and socially disrupted. The place had been built after the war to house families cleared from Glasgow slums. The decline of shipyards and steel mills created widespread unemployment in the community. European Community reports described Easterhouse as resembling more the Third World than the developed West. More than 50 percent of men were unemployed. Substance abuse among the young was common, often leading to tragic deaths.

The company invested £1 million to establish the soap factory, which provides steady employment for 200 people. A quarter of the profits are plowed back into the community through a community-run trust fund. The company also sponsored a drive to build a playground for children.

In 1988, the company launched a paper-making project in Nepal. This project provides employment for dozens of people, many of them women. It has revived the dormant traditional craft of handmade paper. Local craftworkers have bought their own factory with the income generated by this project. The company also established a traveling medical clinic to treat the eye diseases widely prevalent in Nepal.

In the Amazon rain forests, the company has established trade links with the Kayapo Indians. The Kayapo community harvests and processes Brazil nuts for use in The Body Shop products. Members also make brightly colored beaded jewelry for sale in the company stores. This arrangement makes the community economically viable with the least intrusion into its culture.

THE DEPARTMENT OF DAMNED GOOD IDEAS

The Body Shop is a company in a different mold. It has a unique vision, an unusual culture, and exceptional employees with missionary motivations. It does not view itself as just another business, but as a business with a social purpose. Social, ecological, and developmental activities provide the motivational energy in this company. Its distinctive management culture encourages a loose structure and collaborative, imaginative, and improvised work relations.

The Department of Damned Good Ideas (DODGI) provides an example of how human relations work in this setting. This department invites creative ideas from everyone in the company. Many of the suggested ideas are put into practice. One such idea was to start a lottery within the company, with 50 percent of the lottery proceeds going to charities.

Another idea that DODGI implemented was recycling the protective backing from sticky labels. These smooth, glossy pieces of paper are shredded and used as packing in gift baskets. Another innovative DODGI idea involves interdepartmental co-operation. If one department cannot find a solution to a problem, another department will brainstorm it with them. The fresh perspective that outsiders bring often leads to new solutions.

SOME LIMITATIONS

This positive description of The Body Shop's environmental efforts does not mean that the company is perfect in all respects. Competitors and observers have criticized and even legally challenged the company for making exaggerated claims about the absolute natural purity of its ingredients, and its no-animal-testing claims. It has successfully defended these legal and rhetorical challenges. Critics have also accused The Body Shop of being alarmist in its environmental and social campaigns and taking simplistic partisan positions on complex and controversial issues.

The premium prices that The Body Shop charges make its products unaffordable to less affluent people. Its products are priced 20 to 40 percent over even brand-name products in some categories. This makes them "products for the rich." This pricing practice may be necessary in a niche market, but it contradicts the company's avowed value of helping the poor.

Despite these rough edges, The Body Shop can be a useful role model for businesses of the future. Indeed, several companies such as Aveda (hair-care products company, Minneapolis), Esprit (clothing company, San Francisco) and Patagonia (clothing company, Ventura, California) have innovated similar organizational approaches to the environment.

However, not all companies can follow this off-beat approach for two reasons. First, The Body Shop acknowledges that it is able to invest so much in social and environmental programs because it is prosperous. If it were not so prosperous, its values might not change, but its investments in social programs would be cut. Basic financial viability is a necessary condition for greening.

A more important reason is the apparent need for charismatic leadership, like that supplied by Anita and Gordon Roddick. Much of the zeal, passion, energy, and enthusiasm of the company comes from these two people. Whether other companies could emulate this, or whether even The Body Shop itself will continue in this missionary mold after the departure of the Roddicks, remains to be seen.

Conclusions

Several attributes of the missionary approach to greening may be distilled from The Body Shop case. Needed are:

1. Clear *values and vision* of environmental responsiveness, shared widely among employees, and *charismatic leaders* who strongly support these values.
2. Employees with *personal commitment* to environmental and social causes.
3. A management culture that encourages *innovation, tolerance, and experimentation*. A work culture that allows the whole individual to function at work.
4. *Financial prosperity* that allows resources to be diverted into environmental and social programs.
5. Use of simple, *low-technology solutions* and *renewable resources* that are inherently less burdensome on the natural environment.

The powerful benefits of missionary greening are apparent in The Body Shop's phenomenal financial success and rapid growth. The company has distinguished itself competitively in an industry with maturing demand. Its environmentalism created a viable market niche. This niche expanded into the mainstream cosmetics industry, with The Body Shop firmly established as a leader. The competitive advantage of greening was effective in many different countries, making the company a global success.

6

Total Systems Approach: Procter & Gamble, Inc.

The greening of Procter & Gamble, Inc., the consumer-goods giant, shows that corporate greening is not simply a fad, a transient phenomenon, or a small market niche. It is possible even in large, mature, main-line companies. Following Procter & Gamble's lead, many large companies are initiating corporate greening.

Procter & Gamble (P&G) operates in 52 countries including the United States. It employs more than 106,000 people worldwide, and its products are found in almost every household in the United States. It manufactures personal care and health care products, food and beverage products, laundry and cleaning agents, and chemicals. It also provides commercial supply services in these product areas. Its products are reliable and well-known and include such household names as Folger's coffee, Tide, Cheer, and Cascade detergents, Cover Girl cosmetics, and Oil of Olay.

P&G's goal is to have every one of its products have the largest market share. It is not far from achieving this goal. In 1990, 50 percent of its products were number one in their respective markets. The majority of the remaining products were among the top three. As shown in the following table, P&G is financially growing.

PROCTER & GAMBLE FINANCIAL SUMMARY

Year	Sales	Net Income	EPS
1993	30.43	−0.65*	−1.11
1992	29.36	1.87	2.62
1991	27.02	1.77	2.46
1990	24.08	1.60	2.25
1989	21.39	1.20	1.78

Sales and net income in $ billions
EPS=Earnings per share in $
*The 1993 net loss resulted from one-time special restructuring charges, together with mandary non-cash accounting. Without these unusual charges, net earnings would have been 11 percent higher than in the previous year.

In the 1990s, P&G faces new strategic challenges. Consumers are demanding better value. There is heavy competition between its brand-name products and less expensive generic products. The rapid expansion of the economies of developing countries poses the new challenge of reinventing entire product categories.

P&G is responding to consumer quest for value by moving to "value pricing" for 90 percent of its products. In this system, promotion funds and other savings are rolled into reduced list prices every day. It is also saving costs through product and package improvements and technological innovations, such as ultra-thin diapers using curly fiber technology, and thick, soft Charmin tissue using a new proprietary technology.

For a company of such size and scope to become environmentally responsive was a major challenge. The company adopted a "total systems approach" to greening. It systematically studied environmental issues confronting it in the use of natural resources, product designs, packaging, production, transportation, and waste management. Then it designed and implemented changes in all parts of its system. Its objective is to move toward long-term ecological sustainability.

P&G's definition of its total system includes not only the P&G organization, but also its key stakeholders, which include its customers, suppliers, retailers, business associates, regulators, communities, and the media. Its greening efforts extend to all these associates within the integrative framework of a *Total Quality Environmental Management* philosophy.

Top management became aware of the need for company-wide transformation in the 1970s, during the early years of modern environmentalism. The rise of environmental awareness and growing environmental problems created public alarm. Consumers became aware of the ecological costs of the "throw-away" consumer society.

In the 1970s, the use of phosphates in detergents caused a controversy. Phosphates were flowing into and polluting water streams. In the 1980s, disposable diapers accumulating in over-flowing landfills caused a public outcry. Similarly, plastics and paper packaging materials discarded by users contributed to the nation's garbage crisis.

P&G realized the importance of ecological concerns and re-sponded to them through a broad process of transformation based on systematic scientific analysis. Throughout the 1970s, it focused on specific environmental problems caused by its prod-ucts, and on energy conservation. In the early 1980s, it em-barked on a systematic process of environmental quality man-agement that has today made it a leader in corporate environmentalism.

EVOLUTION OF ENVIRONMENTAL CONCERNS

P&G annual reports from 1971, 1972 and 1973 exemplify the balance P&G seeks between consumer responsiveness, product quality, environmental protection, and market shares. The 1971

Annual Report identified phosphates in laundry detergents as "one of the most vexing problems" facing P&G. Consumers were demanding non-phosphate cleaning products. Many American companies were more than ready to jump on the bandwagon. Competitors came out with phosphate-free detergents with much less cleaning power.

P&G research showed that these detergents were too weak to clean effectively. They were also too corrosive to be safe for household use. Instead of selling such products, P&G initiated research on better non-phosphate products. It encouraged consumers not to accept the inferior detergents.

In 1972, Miami, Buffalo and Chicago banned phosphate-based products, and in 1973 the state of Indiana banned them. P&G accepted the reduction in sales, but refused to sell the inferior phosphate-free products—users had come to realize the inferiority. Also, research during this period suggested that the removal of phosphates alone from detergents would do little to clean the nation's water supply.

By 1973, P&G had invested $130 million in phosphate research. It developed a phosphate-free detergent better than any being offered on the market at that time. This product cut the phosphate content of all P&G products by half within one year.

This tenacious pursuit of environmental solutions and faith in scientific research is also reflected in P&G's redesign of packages. The company spends more than $1.4 billion in packaging every year. This huge volume of packaging offered the company great scope for improving its environmental performance. Eco-friendly packaging allows reduction in transportation costs and in the use of fossil fuels for transport. It can lower storage costs, energy use, construction of storage facilities, and reduce wastes sent to landfills.

The company's European operations spearheaded packaging changes in the mid-1980s. German consumers, concerned about municipal solid waste, demanded more eco-friendly packaging. P&G responded with extensive research on product and packaging redesign. It test-marketed Lenor, a concentrated fabric softener, in a refill pouch. Consumers could mix the concentrate with water at home to produce four gallons of the softener. The only waste generated was a small PET plastic pouch with a polyethylene sealant. The Lenor bottle itself was reusable. This product, the equivalent of the Downy fabric softener marketed in the United States, became an immediate success. The new package and concentrated product eliminated the need to discard large four-gallon bottles. This success spurred the company to redesign other products and packages.

ENVIRONMENTAL QUALITY VISION: SATISFYING CONSUMER NEED

The P&G vision of greening is part of the company's mission of satisfying consumer needs. Its "statement of purpose" says:

> We will provide products of superior quality and value that best fill the needs of the world's consumers.
>
> We will achieve that purpose through an organization and a working environment which attracts the finest people; fully develops and challenges our individual talents; encourages our free and spirited collaboration to drive the business ahead; and maintains the Company's historic principles of integrity, and doing the right thing.
>
> Through the successful pursuit of our commitment, we expect our brands to achieve leadership share and profit positions and that, as a result, our business, our people, our shareholders, and the communities in which we live and work, will prosper.

A quote from P&G's "beliefs into action" illustrates its commitment to social responsibility:

> Corporations have a responsibility beyond their basic economic function, just like any U.S. citizen. Their success in achieving their economic goals not only makes it pos-

sible for corporations to create jobs, pay taxes, provide a return to shareholders and develop new and better performing products, it also helps them support other broad needs of society such as education, the arts, and health and social programs.

Guided by this broad vision of social responsibility, P&G developed an environmental quality policy and mission statement in 1989. This policy formalized the ongoing environmental efforts of the company. It provides the guiding framework for greening. The policy includes environmental issues related to products, production, waste, regulations, and technology worldwide. It links these issues to all key stakeholders, reflecting the company's total systems approach. The P&G "environmental quality policy" states:

> *Procter & Gamble is committed to providing products of superior quality and value that best fill the needs of the world's consumers. As a part of this, Procter & Gamble continually strives to improve the environmental quality of its products, packaging, and operations around the world.*
>
> *To carry out this commitment, it is Procter & Gamble's policy to:*
>
> - *Ensure its products, packaging, and operations are safe for our employees, consumers, and the environment.*
> - *Reduce or prevent the environmental impact of its products and packaging in their design, manufacture, distribution, use and disposal whenever possible.*
>
> *We take a leading role in developing innovative, practical solutions to environmental issues related to our products, packaging, and processes. We support the sustainable use of resources and actively encourage reuse, recycling, and composting. We share experiences and expertise and offer assistance to other who may contribute to progress in achieving environmental goals.*

- *Meet or exceed the requirements of all environmental laws and regulations.*

We use environmentally sound practices, even in the absence of governmental standards. We cooperate with governments in analyzing environmental issues and developing cost effective, scientifically based solutions and standards.

- *Continually assess our environmental technology and programs and monitor progress toward environmental goals.*

We develop and use state-of-the-art science and product life cycle assessment, from raw materials through disposal, to assess environmental quality.

- *Provide its consumers, customers, employees, communities, public interest groups, and others with relevant and appropriate factual information about the environmental quality of P&G products, packaging, and operations.*

We seek to establish and nurture open, honest and timely communications and strive to be responsive to concerns.

- *Ensure every employee understands and is responsible and accountable for incorporating environmental quality considerations in daily business activities.*

We encourage, recognize, and reward individual and team leadership efforts to improve environmental quality. We also encourage employees to reflect their commitment to environmental quality outside of work.

- *Have operating policies, programs, and resources in place to implement its environmental quality policy.*

There is widespread commitment to this policy. One reason is that the policy's main proponents are employees and middle management. It was their initiative, and the blessing of then-

CEO John Smale, that led to this policy, which has brought environmental responsiveness to center stage at P&G.

The decentralized business-unit structure of P&G facilitated implementation of the policy. P&G is divided into 34 business units or profit centers. Managers in each unit are responsible for developing their own environmental programs.

This decentralized decision-making authority empowered lower and middle managers to make their own decisions. It encouraged and motivated the entire organization to do something positive about environmental problems. Many of these employees were already aware of the many environmental problems facing their own communities. The environmental policy gave them an opportunity to address these problems through their work. Thus, organizationally, it was the fortuitous combination of top management support, coupled with lower and middle management enthusiasm for environmental programs, that moved the entire company toward environmental responsiveness.

TQEM: TOTAL QUALITY ENVIRONMENTAL MANAGEMENT

The Total Quality Environmental Management (TQEM) system guides P&G's environmental management. This system applies the principles of total quality management to the environment across the entire corporation. TQEM emphasizes several basic ideas. First, that "the customer is always right." The customers are the agents to whom the company must answer on environmental issues. They include local, national, and global environmental rights groups, environmental regulators and environmentally concerned consumers, investors, and employees. The most important customer, however, is the natural environment itself. TQEM gives high priority to preserving and enhancing its integrity.

Another important element of the TQEM system is continuous improvement. TQEM works on the principle that no matter how good you are, you can always be better. TQEM is constantly making efforts to improve environmental performance. A Plan-Do-Check-Act (PDCA) chart is used for improving performance. Employees must be motivated to seek innovative solutions and alternatives. They know that there is no end point in the process, only continual change.

Each project the company undertakes is carefully analyzed so that the job can be done right the first time. This reduces waste, reduces the need for crisis control, and avoids raising the cost of products. Eliminating excess waste reduces the ecological effects of the company's activities.

The final element of the TQEM system is interaction and teamwork. TQEM is structured in teams, each in charge of an environmental project. Teams use fishbone charts and Pareto charts to track, analyze, find the root causes of, and solve problems. Teams also work together to use "benchmarking," or measuring their performance against the best of outside practice. They are encouraged to share ideas and information within the company, within the industry, and within corporate partnerships. They set collective standards for environmental performance. They use "best in the class" examples to set goals.

P&G effectively uses the TQEM system in dealing with its wastewater problem. Viewing nature as a customer of publicly owned treatment works, it tries to minimize the ecological impacts of wastewater. It encourages the development of new wastewater management strategies. Foamy and hot water emitted by production plants represents waste of water, materials, and heat. TQEM guides the analysis of wastewater content, treatment options, and opportunities for using recovered products. The company recovers clean water and reusable heat by using the simple technologies of heat absorption, filtration, and sedimentation.

TQEM also raises environmental issues to strategic levels in the organization. P&G developed corporate strategies that facilitate the creation of environmental programs. Its business strategy involves a strong brand-management system. To maintain strong brands it conducts continual research and development to achieve product excellence.

Brand managers are responsible for all aspects of their brand's performance, including environmental and health performance. They have the freedom to design product, packaging, advertising, pricing, and distribution of their brands. This brand management system allows managers to incorporate environmental and health concerns into early stages of product development.

The strong research and development support and striving for product excellence foster good environmental performance. Company laboratories continuously seek to develop scientific solutions to environmental problems. Management then distributes the best environmental solutions throughout the company, worldwide.

P&G's environmental responsiveness has permeated all parts of the organization. Having green products and packaging was not enough. To be credible to consumers, the company made environmental responsiveness the cornerstone of its strategy. It systematically oriented its inputs, throughput systems, and outputs to ecological sustainability. The changes were systemwide, and brought both competitive gains and long-term improvements in performance.

GREENING OF INPUTS: RESOURCES AND ENERGY

P&G makes a broad range of products, using diverse raw materials. It cannot follow a single materials requirement policy. However, it restricts the use of controversial materials where alternatives are available. It also encourages the use of recycled inputs where possible. In choosing environmentally sound designs and materials, it makes compromises and trade-offs. The company makes these trade-offs through scientific analysis, giving safety and functionality top priority. It makes a special effort to conserve natural resources and energy.

Natural Resources

P&G is a large user of forest resources. It strives continually to reduce the amount of natural resources used. It developed a technology that replaced a significant amount of the wood pulp in disposable diapers with a super-absorbent gel. The resulting diapers weigh less, cost less to transport, and require less land-fill space.

Until 1990, P&G owned its own forests and practiced sustainable yield forestry by harvesting less than 3 percent of its forests each year. It returned more trees to the earth per annum than it used. Extensive research on the development of disease-resistant trees and faster growing seedlings enabled the company to rebuild forests quickly. In France, Holland, and Switzerland, P&G has helped finance tree-planting drives by matching individual gifts from the public.

P&G has joined a number of outside groups in an effort to preserve the forests and wild lands. Along with the Nature Conservancy, it has worked to preserve more than 97,000 acres of wilderness along the Gulf coast of southern Florida. Once owned by P&G, these lands were donated or sold at a discount to the Conservancy.

P&G has supported wildlife preservation projects along the Swannee and Eastern Tallahassee rivers, and has developed new methods for protecting water supplies and wildlife in P&G-owned areas. When setting up a paper products plant in central Pennsylvania, the company hired an outside expert to test the waters of the Susquehanna River and monitor its pollution control system. It invested $30 million into pollution control and remediation equipment to eliminate industrial pollution from the river.

Energy Conservation

Since the oil crisis in the 1970s, P&G has established many energy conservation programs. It encourages the use of energy-efficient buildings. It does preventive maintenance on light fixtures and electric equipment. Its energy conservation programs have targeted two of its most energy-intensive products—paper and dry detergents. Waste pulp from paper mills is converted into pellets and burned as fuel. In another effort to conserve energy, P&G uses co-generation to generate energy and reuse the steam for heating. Burning waste products is another source of energy for several P&G plants. These programs have reduced energy costs from 4 to 2 percent of production costs.

ECOLOGICAL ENERGY SYSTEM

IN NEED OF ENERGY, ZENO GOES TO WINDOW (A), RAISING BLIND (B), ALLOWING SUN TO MELT BLOCK OF ICE (C). WATER DRIPS INTO PAN (D) AND THROUGH TUBE (E) INTO BUCKET (F). WEIGHT OF BUCKET PULLS CORD (G), DRIVING HAMMER (H) INTO SCISSORS (I) AND CUTTING STRING (J) CAUSING WEIGHT (K) TO DROP INTO NET (L). HANDLE OF NET SWINGS UP INTO BULLSEYE (M) MAKING CACTUS (N) FALL ON AND BURST WATER-FILLED BALLOON (O). WATER DOUSES CAT (P) WHO LEAPS FORWARD, PULLING ON STRING (Q) ATTACHED TO LEVER (R), CAUSING BOOT (S) TO SWING UP AND SUDDENLY **ENERGIZE** ZENO.

Source: Unknown.

GREENING OF THROUGHPUTS:
THE PRODUCTION PROCESS

Production plants have undergone a sea change on environmental issues. Twenty years ago, little attention was paid to environmental problems. Ten years ago, environmental issues were the responsibility of an environment staff. Today, all employees feel responsible for what happens to the environment. Most plants have environmental team leaders in each department. Environmental awareness training and responsibility have been driven down to line operators.

An important feature of plant-level environmental programs is transferring "best practices" to plants worldwide. For example, a P&G soap plant in Venezuela devised a production process to deal with water shortages in an arid environment. There was not enough water pressure in the municipal water supply lines to get it up the hill where the plant was located, and there were no sewers to discharge the wastewater. So the plant operators devised a zero-discharge water recycling system. Their techniques were shared with P&G plants around the world.

P&G helped establish the Global Environmental Management Initiative (GEMI). This is the collaborative effort of 20 environmentally concerned companies described in Chapter 3. George D. Carpenter, director of Environment, Energy and Safety Systems at P&G, was the first chairman of GEMI. P&G contributes its positive examples of environmentally sustainable policies and management to GEMI. In turn, GEMI promotes the use of P&G's Total Quality Environmental Management.

GREENING OUTPUTS

Green Products: Design for the Environment

P&G has an internal product and packaging development process that minimizes the environmental impact of its packaging. The process begins by identifying consumer needs and preferences. Using consumer surveys, focus groups, and other market research techniques, product designers identify functional, aesthetic, and environmentally desirable attributes of products and packages. Products/packages are designed to deliver these attributes. Product specifications are finalized after several iterations of design, prototype development, and market testing. Before launch, products are tested by peer groups for safety and environmental concerns. This entire process takes two to five years.

The result of this process of designing for the environment is a large number of environmentally sound products. The list below describes examples of them. P&G is trying to incorporate this system into all its product and packaging design.

Crest Toothpaste. The Crest Neat Squeeze is another dispenser choice in addition to the traditional tube and pump. This new package weighs 50 percent less and has 30 percent less volume than the current pump.

Downy Refill. This small carton of Downy concentrate uses 75 percent less packaging material than the 64-ounce full-strength Downy fabric softener. It was designed to address source reduction by limiting trash generated in the home. The refill carton allows consumers to reuse the large 64-ounce plastic Downy bottle, which is now made of 25 percent recycled plastic.

Secret and Sure "Cartonless." Outside packaging and cartons for these products have been eliminated through new package design. This means a solid waste reduction of 80 million cartons or 3.4 million pounds annually.

Vidal Sassoon Airspray. This is the first and only refillable hair spray that sprays like aerosols—providing a dry, fine mist—but does not use any of the propellants (which deplete ozone) used in traditional hair sprays. This reduces the use of volatile organic compounds by 30 percent, compared to traditional aerosols.

Always Ultra. This sanitary pad uses 40 percent less fiber and is 60 percent lower in volume than conventional maxi pads. Packaging for the product uses 40 percent less material.

Folger's. The "Vacket" package for office food services contains 30 percent less plastic than the conventional pouch package. The flash roasting and flaking process makes the brew leave 30 percent less coffee grounds for disposal.

Frymax Oil. Food service operations can change their deep-frying oil less frequently because of Frymax's longer fry life. This means less oil waste and less packaging. A typical restaurant using 10 cases of liquid shortening per week could reduce oil waste by 38 percent and packaging waste by 15 percent with Frymax.

WASTE MANAGEMENT

P&G pioneered several technologies to reduce waste and improve the performance of its products. Its Superabsorbents technology reduces materials used in disposable diapers and sanitary pads by up to 50 percent. Dehydration is used to reduce detergent bulk (through refills) and packaging (by 30 percent). Compression packaging allows cardboard cartons to be replaced with plastic. This reduces the material used per package by 80 percent. This replacement involved complex trade-offs between different environmental benefits and impacts, however, since plastic comes from a non-renewable resource—petroleum.

P&G's environmental vision includes reducing waste to an absolute minimum through the cooperation of all stakeholders.

It has an integrated solid waste management policy that combines recycling, reuse, and composting. Using landfills is regarded as a last resort.

Composting

Taking cues from successful European programs, P&G promotes composting as an important part of any municipal solid waste program. It educates the public about the benefits of composting—up to 60 percent of materials in landfills can be composted. At the beginning of 1993, there were 20 municipal composting facilities in the United States. Another 200 facilities are in various stages of planning.

P&G pledged $20 million to solid waste composting projects. With these funds, it is helping develop the infrastructure that will make composting feasible for communities. P&G is involved in end-use research for composted materials. With the U.S. Bureau of Mines, P&G is investigating the uses of compost as a means of recovering stripped lands. It is working with the University of Minnesota and the University of Geissen to establish the usefulness of compost as a soil additive for corn and barley crops.

For years consumers demanded biodegradable diapers. P&G diapers are up to 90 percent biodegradable. However, the company does not exploit this fact. It knows that biodegradation does not occur effectively in air- and water-tight landfills. Hence, it developed a disposable diaper that is 80 percent compostable. It is currently developing a fully compostable back sheet for diapers. When implemented, this will create a diaper that is almost completely compostable.

In preparation P&G is creating more composting facilities. It is working with waste management officials in New York, Boston, and San Francisco—three of the largest solid waste producers in the nation—to make plans for composting sites. This attention to the total system (of raw materials, product design, waste management, and reuse of composted materials) is characteristic of the company's TQEM approach.

Source Reduction

Realizing that composting is only one part of an integrated waste management program, P&G has focused on source reduction. In some countries, such as Germany, families pay a weekly fee per pound of garbage disposed of. To minimize garbage, P&G offers products in refill pouches. It has enlisted the help of bottle makers to develop an international labeling system for recyclable bottles.

Waste management at production plants is part of the TQEM program. Each facility is responsible for minimizing emissions and wastes. Continuous surveillance is maintained through the monthly reports sent to the corporate environmental department.

P&G seeks to create an "industrial ecology" around its plants. In this system, waste from one plant is used as raw material for a neighboring plant. Quality improvement engineers at plants continually seek opportunities to sell their wastes. They actively engage in creating new markets for their own wastes and becoming users of others' wastes.

INFRASTRUCTURE AND STAKEHOLDER PARTNERSHIP NETWORKS

The systems approach used by P&G extends to outside agencies in industry, government, and community. It has established creative partnerships with external stakeholders to leverage its environmental programs. Its partnerships promote environmental education, legislation, environmental programs in supplier firms, working with retailers, and industry cooperation.

Environmental Education

The company works closely with schools to promote environmental education. It provides educators with innovative teaching aids on rain forests. One program uses the movie *The Medicine*

Man to create a series of rain forest education aids. Activities are designed to make students aware of their dependence on the Brazilian rain forest. They show how their chewing gum, their raincoats, their sugar, and their sneakers all originated in the rain forest. Students realize that these daily items could be lost. They begin understanding the complex interdependencies and fragility of natural environments, and are motivated to preserve them. The program educates students on how to go about this preservation.

Legislative Actions

P&G works with legislators at state and national levels to create practical legislation. Since 1988, it has actively worked with the Coalition of Northeastern Governors (CONEG) and the Source Reduction Council to frame environmental legislation. The company shares its scientific and technological knowledge to help create rational and practical regulations. It works closely with legislators, participates in public/private discussions, and engages environmental groups in creating regulations. CONEG's heavy metals bill is derived directly from P&G's internal policy on heavy metals. Its success has attracted some criticism from other businesses. They feel P&G "collaborates with the enemy" to regulate industry.

Supplier Support

P&G works with suppliers to ensure a continuous supply of high quality supplies and particularly recycled materials. It helped establish a stable market for recycled plastics. It invested in solving technological problems associated with reprocessing plastics. It also works with suppliers to develop appropriate packaging. It encourages virgin plastics manufacturers to produce recyclable materials and recycled resins.

P&G's relationships with suppliers are highly interactive. It maintains open two-way communication and mutual learning relationships from which both parties benefit. It now has fewer and more reliable suppliers to whom it offers longer contracts (three to four years), in order to standardize and maintain quality. This supplier relationship has allowed the company to employ recycled fiber for 80 percent of the 1.5 billion paper cartons it uses each year.

Working with Resellers

P&G works closely with wholesalers and retailers to create environmental awareness in the distribution system. Its programs focus on energy-efficient warehousing and minimizing losses in storage and transportation. It also has a product integrity system that includes clear product labeling for safety, customer education, redistribution of excess perishable foods, and truthful "green" advertising.

P&G believes that long-term solutions to environmental problems must include changes in customers' habits. Consumers must move toward responsible buying. They must support recycled-goods markets. They must participate in recycling and composting. In conjunction with retailers, the company established the "Keep America Beautiful" and "Let's Not Waste the 90s" programs. Using customer education and buying incentives (discounts), these programs encourage customers to recycle and reduce wastes.

Industry Cooperation

P&G has considerable influence in industry to encourage other companies to adopt environmentally sound policies. GEMI is one example of its efforts to promote good environmental practices globally. It has also urged companies to voluntarily adopt CONEG's Preferred Packaging Guidelines. It works with the Food Manufacturing Institute, the National Food Processors Association, and the Grocery Manufacturers Association to develop environmental guidelines and standards for the industry. It has joined several other companies to create the Solid Waste Composting Council to promote composting.

COMPANY IMAGE

These systematic environmental activities give P&G a definitive green image. However, in a large and complex company such as this, there are many social and environmental issues that can be criticized. Consumer product companies, including P&G, spend enormous amounts of money on advertising. This encourages overconsumption, which is not ecologically sustainable on a global scale. P&G also produces many ecologically unsustainable products. For example, however "green" one makes disposable diapers, their ecological sustainability is questionable. The very idea of "disposability" contradicts the eco-centric premise of recycling.

In the past, there have been instances of clashes between environmentalists and workers at P&G plants. The company tries to avert such conflicts, and by and large succeeds. It seeks to maintain harmonious community relations. Yet, given the many different and complex communities in which it operates worldwide, these relations have not been uniformly harmonious.

In recent years, P&G was castigated for becoming more rigid, spying on employees, and forcing conformity. Ed Artzt, the CEO, was portrayed as being too autocratic. Part of this may be a response to the threat from non-branded generic products, the size of which caught the company unawares. In response it initiated cost-cutting programs that alienated many employees.

LESSONS TO BE LEARNED

From this detailed look at all aspects of P&G's greening, other companies can learn several lessons.

1. *Scientific research and technological innovation* in designing products, packaging and production are key sources of environmental solutions.

2. An *integrated systems approach* that covers all aspects of organization-environment relations is critical for success. Such an approach prevents shifting of environmental costs/risks from one medium or process to another. It leads to a reduction of total environmental impact. It also prevents arbitrary externalizing of environmental costs.

3. *Grass-roots employee support and middle-management support* for environmental efforts is critical to energizing the company. Many employees want to be environmentally responsible. By giving them opportunities, incentives, and rewards to do so, companies can initiate environmental programs with little effort.

4. After initiations, environmental efforts should be made *systematic and standard* for efficient operations. Since environmental technologies and solutions are new and evolving, there is scope for *continuous improvement* in these programs.

5. *Involvement of external stakeholders* in environmental efforts is also critical. Consumers, suppliers, distributors, and regulators affect many aspects of firm–environment relations. Their cooperation is essential if the company wishes to make an impact on its total environment.

6. The *Total Quality Environmental Management* approach is a useful way of extending quality-management programs to ecological problems. It strives to achieve zero pollution through continuous improvement and periodic measurement of environmental performance.

Green Trading: Loblaw International Merchants

7

The Body Shop and Procter & Gamble exemplify the greening of companies that manufacture and sell their own products. What about companies that sell only products made by others? Such companies do not control raw-material choices, energy consumption, pollution, and waste from manufacturing plants.

This is the case for the retailing industry—one of the largest sectors of the American economy. Retailing is essentially a trading business. It involves buying, storing, transporting, and selling goods, with little if any manufacturing. Can retailers be environmentally responsive?

Loblaw International Merchants, Inc. (called Loblaw) of Toronto gives a resoundingly affirmative answer to this question. In the mundane world of grocery supermarkets, Loblaw has created a unique business. The main tool it uses is "green trading."

In 1989, Loblaw introduced its President's Choice G.R.E.E.N. product line. These products, friendly to the environment, constitute 15 percent of the products sold by the company. This has propelled the company to a position of environmental leadership in the industry.

Grocery retailing is a low-margin business. Companies in this industry make only pennies on every invested dollar. In contrast, Loblaw has double-digit growth and profitability.

PREREQUISITES FOR GREENING: CONSUMER ORIENTATION AND GREEN DEMAND

The heart of Loblaw greening is its astute product differentiation and marketing. Green marketing caters to the emerging green orientation of consumers and demand for green products. The former allows the company to see market opportunities, and the later creates market opportunities.

Brand management is an important part of the Loblaw greening strategy. Loblaw introduced No-Name (generic) brands in 1978. Customers were very happy with these inexpensively priced products. By 1980, 80 percent of its customers had tried generics. Another 35 percent were buying at least five generic products per store visit.

Surprisingly, the company found that the generic product buyers were generally more affluent and educated. They were looking for *good values* and did not need brand names to validate their purchase decisions. Loblaw targeted this higher income group for its President's Choice line, launched in 1984.

The President's Choice line gave customers unique value. It had products of exceptional quality at a moderate price (not the lowest price). Examples of these included "The Decadent" chocolate chip cookie, Devonshire custard from England, Russian mustard, and other upscale gourmet foods. The Decadent cookies competed with the leading brand name, "Chips Ahoy," from RJR Nabisco. The Decadent cookies contained double as many chocolate chips as their rival, and were made with pure butter. They became an immediate success and far outsold Chips Ahoy.

In establishing the President's Choice line, the company developed some unique internal support systems and management processes. It gained product development expertise, a worldwide vendor network, and new merchandising skills. Two internal groups, Loblaw International Merchants (LIM) and Loblaw Intersave Group (LIG), worked together to develop and merchan-

Source: Reprinted with special permission of King Features Syndicates.

dise this new line. By 1989, 30 percent of Loblaw's total grocery sales came from 2,200 generic products and 700 President's Choice products.

By the late 1980s, the "value" idea seemed to have run its course in the company's brand-management strategy. It was also being copied by competitors. This is when Loblaw's president, David Nichols, and his group of managers came up with the idea of the G.R.E.E.N. line as an extension of President's Choice.

In his travels to Europe, Nichols had noticed the success of *The Green Consumer Guide*. He became aware of Germany's Blue Angel environmental certification program. He was impressed by The Body Shop's green strategy. Public opinion polls in Canada had repeatedly shown the public's growing concern about environmental degradation. Loblaw's own consumer surveys showed great demand for environmentally friendly and "body-friendly" products.

THE G.R.E.E.N. PRODUCT LINE

Nichols did not have a great vision of saving the earth with green products. At the launch of the G.R.E.E.N. line in June 1989, he simply said:

> "We acknowledge that we are not environmental experts and we readily admit that we do not have all the answers. However, we feel strongly that these products are a step in the long journey towards the solution of our enormous environmental problems. If G.R.E.E.N. products do nothing more than help raise awareness of the need to address environmental issues now, and give Canadians hope that something can be done, then in the end, they will have made a positive contribution."

The G.R.E.E.N. line was a market opportunity that happened to be environmentally sound. Extensive R&D preceded its launching. Loblaw consulted environmental groups to identify environmentally friendly products and packaging. The company worked with leading Canadian environmental groups such as Pollution Probe and Friends of the Earth to determine product specifications and packaging designs. Pollution Probe helped with testing products and even certified their environmentally friendly features.

These products included unbleached, recycled paper products (bathroom tissues, disposable diapers, coffee filters, and sanitary napkins). Eliminating bleaching eliminated the use of toxic chlorine, furans, and dioxins that are a major source of pollution. Using recycled paper reduced use of virgin paper by 50 percent.

To promote the use of environmentally better products, the G.R.E.E.N. line also included existing products that were more environmentally friendly than alternatives. Products thus placed under the G.R.E.E.N label included recycled motor oil, phosphate-free detergents, child-safe bitter-tasting cleaning products, and baking soda for cleaning purposes.

In a variation of The Body Shop strategy, Loblaw also introduced "body-friendly" products. These included low-cholesterol, low-fat products such as "Virtuous Cooking Spray," which contained canola oil and came in a CFC-free container. "Virtuous Soda Crackers" had no cholesterol and low salt. "Leaner Than Lean" meats had low fat content and came in smaller-size servings. "Vitari Frozen Fruit Dessert" was an ice cream substitute with no cholesterol, lactose, added sugar, or artificial flavors and colors.

The company offered salad dressings with all-natural ingredients, containing no MSG. It promoted the use of olive oil, high fiber and bran products, preservative-free products, and natural foods. Pesticide-free foods were introduced, such as Cox's Orange Pippin Apple Juice made from Alar-free apples. The company offered "If the World Were Perfect" water, which was purified by a reverse-osmosis process. Today, Loblaw offers more than 110 products in the G.R.E.E.N. line, accounting for more than $100 million in revenues.

But offering green products alone, while continuing to pollute and destroy the environment otherwise, did not seem consistent. Environmentalists and consumers would see the contradictions in a company that had green products but black chimneys. Loblaw realized that partial greening was not feasible. It embarked on a corporate-wide environmental audit to identify and deal with environmental issues in all parts of the company.

THE TOTAL GREENING OF LOBLAW

The environmental audit reviewed the company's environmental performance against regulations. It included environmental impact assessments of new projects. It developed an environmental action plan, identifying many opportunities for changing product designs, packaging, recycling, energy conservation, and using recycled materials. It recommended changes in production processes and vendor management. In response, the company initiated programs in all these areas.

Since Loblaw does not own production facilities, it avoids industrial pollution, chemical emissions, and industrial wastes. Its energy conservation programs minimize energy consumption. These programs include heat- and light-efficient building designs, preventive maintenance, and eliminating wasteful energy use.

A key benefit of this systematic environmental impact assessment was the development of a Resource, Environment and Waste Management Policy in 1990. This policy provides the guiding framework for greening the company. It complies with all environmental regulations. It establishes environmental performance monitoring systems and annual review and evaluation procedures. It calls for use of the best available technological and economic solutions to environmental problems. It makes senior management accountable for environmental performance. It gives the board of directors explicit responsibility for conducting an annual review of environmental performance. It also provides detailed implementation guidelines.

Product changes are the fundamental element of a green strategy for a grocery firm. There are thousands of products that the company deals with and they come from an equally large number of vendors. Loblaw's product design and purchasing departments work with vendors to reform existing products and make them environmentally sound. They also design new eco-friendly products.

This process is full of trade-offs and compromises. Each design choice involves some improvement on one environmental criterion, yet may have unintended detrimental effects on another. For example, replacing Styrofoam with paper or plastic reduces the need for ozone-depleting chlorofluorocarbons (CFCs). However, paper and plastic use up trees and non-renewable petroleum. They require more energy to produce and pose different disposal problems. To deal with this complexity, Loblaw's consumer-products department provides information about environmental trade-offs directly to consumers. This way consumers can make more informed choices.

Loblaw has also taken its environmentalism outside the company. It has established environmental partnerships with communities, with suppliers, environmentalists, and government agencies. It supports environmental awareness projects in the communities where it operates. It works with suppliers to carry out environmental audits of their operations and design environmentally friendly products. It works with environmental groups in order to update itself continually on trends and new ideas for environmental programs. Loblaw executives frequently lecture at colleges and at civic and professional business meetings to share their experience with others. They work with government agencies to develop regulations and codes of practice for the whole industry.

IMPACT ON STAKEHOLDERS

How successful are Loblaw's greening efforts? There is no simple answer to this question. Their greening has had positive affects on many stakeholders. It has also created controversies and vigorous debates among consumers, environmentalists, business representatives, and government agencies.

Positive Impact

The company has reaped public respect for trying to deal constructively with environmental issues. The media reported on Loblaw's efforts in a positive light. Loblaw executives received many invitations for television and public presentations of their story. Government agencies in charge of environmental, health, and safety issues saw Loblaw as a leader in greening and supported the company's efforts.

Loblaw's green strategy has had a definite effect on profitability. Consumers have accepted the strategy enthusiastically. Within four weeks of launch, 82 percent of customers were aware of the G.R.E.E.N. product line and 27 percent had bought G.R.E.E.N. products. The product line has continued to grow since its introduction. It contributed $100 million in revenues in 1991.

The green strategy provided the company with a distinct competitive advantage over other grocery chains in Canada. It offered consumers a better set of options. Deeply committed environmental consumers switched to even cursorily green products offered by the company. Loblaw's market share in the grocery business has gone up 2 percent since introduction of the G.R.E.E.N. line. Customers are attracted to company stores by the line. Once in the store, they stay and buy other groceries as well. This broad consumer acceptance led many competitors to copy Loblaw products and packaging.

Negative Impact

In the environmentalist and consumer-activist communities, the G.R.E.E.N. line received mixed reviews. Greenpeace launched an attack on Loblaw's "organic fertilizer," denouncing it as potentially toxic, and asking for its withdrawal from the market. (Agriculture Canada rigorously tested the product and gave a favorable opinion on it.) Consumers Association of Canada said that Loblaw was misleading consumers. It disputed the company's claim that its disposable diapers were beneficial to the environment, and that its unsalted crackers were healthier than others on the market. Pollution Probe had earlier endorsed both these products. In the ensuing controversy, the president of Pollution Probe resigned. The group also withdrew its endorsements of the products.

Employee Empowerment

Perhaps the most important impact of the green strategy has been to give employees at Loblaw the freedom to initiate environmental projects. Through its pro-environment values and commitments, the company encourages employee environmentalism. In this pro-environment culture, employees have come up with innovative initiatives, including recycling programs and an environmental information service for consumers.

A store manager came up with the idea of eliminating grocery bags altogether by redesigning shopping carts. The new system will use shopping carts with removable, returnable recycled plastic boxes. Shoppers will sort groceries directly into these boxes, as they pick them from the shelves. The boxes would be taken home and returned later. This system will increase margins by 0.5 percent and eliminate grocery bags. The company is experimenting with different versions of this system.

Clearly, Loblaw's environmental efforts are impressive. Initiated as a product brand strategy, they now cover all aspects of the company. The strategy paid off in terms of consumer response, competitive benefits, and improved business performance. This narrow strategy mushroomed within the company to engulf all operations. Now it has taken root in voluntary initiatives by employees.

Despite these impressive gains, Loblaw has a long way to go in becoming a fully environmentally sustainable company. In 1992, its G.R.E.E.N. products accounted for $100 million of $8.5 billion in revenues—less than 1.5 percent. To build credibility for its environmental efforts, the company needs to increase the proportion of green products on its shelves. It may not be feasible to make all the company's products environmentally sound. What is important is to put into place organizational policies, values, and systems that move the company in that direction.

LESSONS TO BE LEARNED

1. Consumers are becoming increasingly sensitive to environmental impacts of products. They are demanding environmentally responsible products and packages. Environmental attributes of products and packages can be a basis of competitive strategies.

2. Marketing variables (product, package, price, promotion, distribution) in general, and brand management in particular, are excellent vehicles for implementing environmental programs.

3. Green marketing claims must be supported by organization-wide greening. Claims must be objectively verifiable. Truth in advertising green claims is essential for long-term credibility.

4. Retailers interested in greening must work closely with suppliers. Suppliers should be encouraged to create environmentally friendly products and packages. Retailers should develop environmentally oriented vendor management policies. These policies must reach deep into vendor organizations to influence product/package specifications, energy and resource conservation, and waste management programs.

5. Judicious use of endorsements by environmental groups and community leaders can be useful in gaining credibility with consumers.

Organic Greening:
Ben & Jerry's Homemade
Ice Creams, Inc.

One bright summer morning I drove up the hillside to the Disneyland-like campus of Ben & Jerry's Homemade Ice Creams, Inc. (B&J) in Waterbury, Vermont. One look at the festively colored buildings made me wonder whether I was overdressed. Having read a lot about the company's unconventional nature, I wore a pair of green trousers and a short-sleeved shirt with a tie. Mitch Curren, the "PR Info Queen," greeted me at the door. She ushered me through the pastel-rainbow-colored lobby to meet the "Green Team," an informal, voluntarily selected, and continually changing group interested in doing environmental projects. It includes employees from all departments, and is responsible for assessing how the company affects the environment in all its areas of operation.

Everyone in the room wore T-shirts, jeans, and sneakers. The running joke at B&J is that when anyone wants to feel well dressed, they just stand next to co-founder Ben Cohen. Mr. Cohen's sartorial style (or lack of it) is legendary. He once accepted a national award for the best small business of the year from President Reagan, wearing a crumpled khaki shirt. The shirt was pulled out of a box from the trunk of his car.

B&J is an unusual company in many respects other than dress code and decor. Its most distinctive feature is its approach to environmental issues. The term "organic" best captures my sense of environmental management at B&J. Environmental efforts occur naturally and effortlessly within the company. Environmental tasks are not separated from operating functions. They are an integral part of everyday activities. Everyone in the company participates. The Green Team is a vehicle for this wide participation. Its membership is continually evolving, and members come from all parts of the company.

Two young men, Ben Cohen and Jerry Greenfield, established B&J in 1978. Their only claim to expertise was a $5 correspondence course on ice-cream making in the home kitchen, and a passion for ice cream. Started from their home kitchen, the company became a national brand, and went public in 1984. By 1992, B&J had grown into a company with $131 million in revenues, about 350 employees, and 100 franchised scoop shops. It had 36 percent of the market share in the super-premium ice-cream segment, a close second to Häagen-Dazs.

BEN & JERRY'S FINANCIAL SUMMARY

Year	Sales	Net Income	EPS
1992	131.96	6.67	1.07
1991	96.99	3.73	0.67
1990	77.02	2.60	0.50
1989	58.46	2.05	0.40
1988	47.56	1.61	0.31
5-yr growth	29.0%	42.5%	36.6%

Sales and net income in $ millions
EPS=Earnings per share in $

This rapid growth is all the more impressive in a mature, extremely competitive industry. During each of the years from 1988 to 1992, ice-cream consumption has remained constant or declined. Until B&J appeared, the super-premium segment of the ice-cream industry was an oligopoly dominated by Häagen-Dazs and Frusen-Gladje. This impressive financial performance is accompanied by equally impressive social and ecological performance.

PRODUCT, SOCIAL, AND ECONOMIC MISSIONS

To understand how environmental efforts became a natural and authentic part of B&J, we need to look at the company's basic values. Both Ben and Jerry were idealists and social activists at heart. Growing up in the 1960s, their values were shaped by a period when social and environmental activism were popular. They started the company not only to make profits but to promote social change. They wanted to support their social and political causes and have fun while doing business. Their original vision for the company was to use business for social change. This vision is a part of the company's mission. It is achieved through product development linked to social causes, organic environmentalism, and green stakeholder programs.

The company has a broad and comprehensive vision of greening. Its mission statement says that the company is dedicated to the creation and demonstration of a "new corporate concept of linked prosperity," prosperity that includes being responsive to environmental, employee, local community, and social needs while still making modest profits. This green vision is best captured in the company's various missions, which include a product mission, a social mission, and an economic mission.

The product mission is simply to "to make, distribute and sell the finest quality all-natural ice cream and related products in a wide variety of innovative flavors made from Vermont dairy products." Its social mission is "to operate the company in a way that actively recognizes the central role that business plays in the structure of society by initiating innovative ways to im-

Source: Reprinted by permission of Ben & Jerry's Homemade Ice Creams, Inc., Waterbury Vermont.

prove the quality of life of a broad community: local, national, and international." The economic mission is "to operate the company on a sound financial basis of profitable growth, increasing value for shareholders and creating career opportunities and financial rewards for employees."

Its strategy is to market premium, very high quality products while promoting a broad social and environmental agenda. Its social programs include Brazilian rain forest conservation, waste management, recycling, the "One Percent for Peace" project, promoting family farms, Native American programs, and a profit donation program—7.5 percent of its pre-tax profits are donated to charity. The company has blended its business and social missions to create a unique green identity, with high customer loyalty and profits.

ICE CREAMS WITH SOCIAL CAUSES

Ice creams are an unlikely product for fostering social revolution. And expensive, fatty, premium-brand ice creams may represent the epitome of social irrelevance. Yet with premium ice creams as its core business, B&J has creatively designed its product to be associated with social causes.

B&J's Wild Maine Blueberry Ice Cream uses wild blueberries picked by the Passamaquoddy of Maine. They harvest and process blueberries on their reservation. B&J buys $330,000 worth of blueberries from them each year. This gives them a steady source of income and makes them self-reliant. Similarly, B&J buys Brazil nuts and cashew nuts grown and harvested by natives of the Amazonian rain forest. By helping them to maintain their traditional lifestyles, the company also helps protect the rain forest.

One of the social causes the company is committed to is supporting family-owned farms. So it buys all its cream from a dairy cooperative of such farms. The Fresh Georgia Peach Light Ice Cream uses peaches from a family farm in Georgia.

B&J buys its candy from Community Projects, Inc., a company that donates its profits to rain forest preservation. (B&J created Community Projects, Inc., as a venture to promote social programs.) It buys brownies from Greystone Bakery, which provides training and employment for homeless people.

"Peace Pops" is another product directly linked to a social cause—world peace. The company donates profits from this product to the "One Percent for Peace" Foundation. The objective of this organization is to divert 1 percent of the Pentagon budget to social programs and international understanding.

This link between social causes and products has several benefits. It provides concrete support to specific causes. It clarifies and shares the company's core values among employees and stakeholders. It also gives the company a progressive social image, which in turn gives competitive advantage in certain segments of the market.

Environmentalism and the "Green Team"

Environmental concerns are an organic part of the company's culture and operations. Environmental actions occur in the company as part of everyday activities. Employees with ideas for environmental and social projects "just do them." The company provides forums for discussing these ideas. Its culture encourages them and supplies resources to implement them.

A manager of natural resources coordinates and facilitates environmental activities. Much of the initiative for such activities comes from individual employees. Employees with environmental ideas become members of the Green Team. The team's mission statement reads: "Dedicated to motivating and communicating a sense of environmental responsibility throughout Ben & Jerry's community by developing and motivating creative earth-respecting programs."

The Green Team meets periodically to plan new actions and assess progress on past ones. Within one 40-minute meeting of the team, I observed its members resolve eight environmental issues. They made decisions about:

- Methods of reusing and recycling cardboard drums used to store ice cream.
- Changing the procedure for picking up recycled paper to improve the recycling rate.
- Participating in a fund raiser for a local youth club.
- Educating themselves and the company on the use of cornstarch polymers, such as Nuvon, for packaging.
- Arranging for the pickup of recycling equipment.
- Doing an environmental education skit for the Quality Council (executive committee of the company).
- Improving reuse of paper used on one side by cutting and binding it into notepads.

For each problem, ideas and solutions were solicited, alternatives were discussed, decisions were made, and volunteers assigned to implement the decision. By the time the meeting ended, several environmental projects had been initiated. The manager for natural resources took responsibility for making the necessary resources available.

The Green Team meets every month to brainstorm environmental issues. The more complicated and technical environmental problems are handed off to other professional groups. These include the E-Team (in charge of the energy program) and the production, maintenance, marketing, and design teams.

B&J's environmental programs try to compensate for all the environmental effects of company operations. They include management of waste streams, conserving energy and resources, exploring sources of sustainable alternative energy, establishing linkages between products and environmental causes, and setting up community environmental awareness programs.

An Integrated Production System

The environmental benefits of products such as Rain Forest Crunch are obvious. More imaginative environmental efforts are focused on the production system. The production of ice cream on a commercial scale is a process that is only modestly polluting. B&J designed a production system that integrates energy conservation, resource management, production, packaging, and waste treatment into a single comprehensive system.

Energy Conservation. The company's goal is to reduce energy consumption by 25 percent over the next five years. Periodic corporate-wide energy audits update energy conservation programs. B&J now uses compact fluorescent lights, low-wattage light bulbs, and variable speed drives for condensers. It has installed occupancy sensors that turn off the lights if a room is vacant for five minutes—this alone will save the company $250,000 per year.

B&J is experimenting with high-efficiency refrigeration systems using outdoor air in the winter. It is testing the feasibility of plants that co-generate energy from waste, and of solar-powered delivery trucks and refrigeration systems.

Resource Conservation. The company's comprehensive *resource conservation* programs involve use reduction, recycling and reuse of office materials, containers, and wastes wherever possible. To maximize the use of raw materials, the company has developed an automated and high-efficiency production system.

Company stationery, copier, computer, and laser-printer paper is unbleached and 100 percent recycled. Double-sided copies are made wherever possible. Office pens are refillable. Printer toner cartridges are recycled and printer ribbons are reinked. Even greeting cards are recycled. Some office paper is reused for animal bedding and packaging. Dishes and flatware in the cafeteria are reused. Reuse of plastic containers for ingredients reduced the amount of cardboard sold for recycling from 1,800 pound/bales per week to 5 pound/bales per week.

Production Wastes. These are similarly recycled. Ten thousand pounds of plastic egg-yolk pails are recycled and reused each year. The milky liquids (untreatable in the local waste plant) left over from ice-cream manufacture are fed to pigs in the local area. The company even bought 200 pigs to keep this waste fully used as feed. B&J uses 500 to 700 gallons of ice cream spillage per day to sweeten farmer's manure pits. Water and flavoring jugs are recycled.

Solid Wastes. B&J minimizes generation of solid waste by designing packaging carefully and reusing plastic and cardboard parts. Any extra-clean used fiberboard boxes are sold to a company that reuses them. To remove pollutants from wastewater, the company set up a pilot wastewater treatment system designed by Solar Aquatics. Working on the greenhouse principle, this system uses solar energy and natural vegetation in an artificial marshland to purify water.

In addition, the company sponsors community projects, campaigns, and events to promote environmental awareness. Examples of these include Vermont's Merry Mulching program to recycle Christmas trees and leftover paint cans. B&J's New Vaudeville Light Circus Bus is crisscrossing the United States offering variety entertainment; it is powered by 180 square feet of photovoltaic cells and symbolizes the feasibility of solar energy. Together with 17 other companies, B&J organized a campaign to support the congressional bill calling for auto fuel efficiency standards of 40 miles per gallon by the year 2000.

In 1992, B&J signed the Valdez Principles, proposed by the Coalition for Environmentally Responsible Economies (CERES). CERES is a coalition of leading businesses, environmental organizations, and institutional investor groups. These comprehensive principles (see Chapter 11 for a listing of them) bind companies to 10 standard environmental practices, including an annual environmental audit. B&J was the largest company to sign this agreement.

An important aspect of B&J's environmental management is the integrity of the process used for resolving problems. This process is voluntary and informal, and connected naturally to company operations, values, and employee preferences. The resulting environmental solutions, while guided by scientific and common-sense analysis are sensitive to implementation barriers. By providing a flexible and open process, the company ensures a high degree of genuine volunteer employee participation.

GREEN STAKEHOLDER PROGRAMS

Another element of B&J's organic greening is its broad conception of company prosperity, which includes the welfare of the many stakeholders and communities associated with it. B&J has established a relationship of mutual responsibility with its key stakeholders, and considers the economic and social concerns of these stakeholders in its strategic decisions. This concern is reflected in its programs for employees, neighboring farmers, the local community, customers, suppliers, and the support of general social causes such as world peace and the natural environment.

Employee Relations. B&J's programs have created a highly committed and loyal work force. Employee wages, benefits, and work conditions are the best in the area. Benefits include the traditional medical, leave, stock ownership, and contributory pension plans. The company has also established some innovative new programs: parental leave and adoption assistance, on-site child care, financial counseling for employees, and a military-leave policy that guarantees jobs and pays salary differentials. It tries to maintain the ratio of entry-level wages to highest salaries of one to seven. The Institutional Shareholder Services, Inc., reported: "In all measures of work life, Ben and Jerry's people have a far more favorable view of their jobs, supervision, and company than do employees from American companies in general."

Supplier Alliances. The company has created alliances with suppliers in the local community and elsewhere. By agreement, it buys milk from local dairy farmers at fixed prices, sometimes above the market rate. Unlike its competitors, the company does not squeeze the farmers: It refrains from buying solely during periods of lower prices. By buying locally and ensuring a steady demand and fair price, it offers economic stability to local dairy farmers. B&J's other supplier alliances contribute to a diverse set of social causes. For example, as noted above, it has long-term supply contracts with Maine's Passamaquoddy, Amazon native tribes in Brazil, and the Greystone Bakery.

Customer Needs. The company is highly responsive to its customers and their needs and preferences. Its leading products are premium ice creams in many innovative flavors. It has created many popular ice creams, including Rain Forest Crunch, Chocolate Fudge Brownie, Wild Maine Blueberry, and Peace Pops. It also produces light ice creams, fruit ices, and frozen yogurts to meet the needs of health-conscious Americans. Realizing the negative health effects of consuming too much fat, the company voluntarily advises its customers to eat ice cream in moderation.

CARING CAPITALISM

Besides integrating social activities into its daily business activities, B&J is redefining business philanthropy. Most progressive companies donate 1 to 2 percent of their pre-tax income to philanthropy. B&J sets aside 7.5 percent of pre-tax profits for distribution to diverse social causes. More important is the way B&J manages this philanthropy. Most companies pass it off to an outside foundation that operates without any participation from the company. Some even apologize to stockholders for putting company profits into social causes. Others see it as a way of buying legitimacy and community goodwill.

Not so with B&J. In 1990 and 1991 the B&J Foundation received contributions of $363,000 and $528,000 respectively from B&J. Jerry Greenfield himself chairs the board of trustees of the B&J Foundation. The foundation also includes many B&J employees. Top management sees it as an extension of the company's social mission; in fact, the company's annual report gives performance information on foundation activities.

Since its beginning in 1985, the foundation has given away $1.5 million to a wide variety of social service groups. Beneficiaries of this philanthropy have included:

- INFACT, a Boston-based activist group currently conducting a boycott campaign against General Electric because of its production of nuclear weapons.
- Farmworker Power Project, a Denver program that trains farm laborers to negotiate work agreements with growers.
- Teamster Rank and File Education and Legal Defense, a Detroit-based project intended to promote democracy in the Teamsters Union.

- The Devastators, an all-children's Afro-American percussion band whose music is focused on combatting AIDS and homelessness, and promoting world peace and environmentalism.
- The Heifer Project, which provides agricultural animals to impoverished communities.
- Worker-Owned Network, which mobilizes community resources for worker cooperatives.
- The Women's Institute for Housing and Development.

The company also, as mentioned earlier, donates 1 percent of pre-tax profits to the "One Percent for Peace" organization, which encourages activities and education that promote world peace, and is seeking ways of converting defense programs into ones that benefit civilians.

ORGANIC GREENING AT BEN & JERRY'S

Organic greening at B&J is based on a broad vision of the company, its environment and its notion of prosperity.

- The company views itself as a business with social objectives. Its concept of the environment includes its stakeholders, associated communities, and the natural environment. Its concept of prosperity is one of shared benefits and long-term sustainability.
- Environmental actions are an integral part of daily operations. They emerge from the informal and open decision processes of a voluntarily formed Green Team.
- Environmental efforts are given focus and guidance through scientific and commonsense analysis. Difficult problems are tackled with scientific and technological innovation, and simple problems with common sense.
- The emphasis is on building environmentally positive linkages and partnerships within and outside the company. The em-

phasis is also on action and accomplishment, with limited resources given to measuring the effects of these actions.

- Greening is a grass-roots effort by employees. The top management is not directly involved in either monitoring or
guiding it. The company founders have made their support
for environmental efforts explicit and empowered employees
to act on their own environmental impulses.

CONCLUSIONS

The "linked prosperity" idea is apparent in B&J's diverse array
of business and social programs. The company has created a
unique web of mutually beneficial and reinforcing relationships
with its key stakeholders. This network provides the competitive
advantage of dedicated, loyal, flexible, accommodating, and
friendly employees and business associates. This is a great asset
in the highly competitive ice-cream industry.

This description of the company's environmental and social
efforts is not to imply that the company is without areas for improvement. While its products are of high quality, they contain
large amounts of fat and sugar. Both these ingredients are
harmful when consumed in excess. The company realizes this
and suggests moderation in consuming ice creams. Such moderation will be encouraged as the company provides more complete
nutrition information on its ice-cream packages.

Another area for improvement is its human resources policies.
The company is generous in giving good wages and benefits to
employees. However, the tasks in automated ice-cream making
are not very challenging. The company attempts to add to job
satisfaction by encouraging employees to engage in community
projects. By increasing such efforts and involving workers in decision making, the company can improve the motivation of
lower-level employees. Its large-scale employment of women is
laudable. Moving these women to top management positions

and hiring more minority employees are areas for further improvement.

As B&J grows, it faces increasing pressures to adopt aggressive sales and financial tactics. It has been criticized for predatory pricing policies that stifle smaller competitors, much in the way that the company itself was stifled when it was small. The pressures to behave like large, established traditional companies will continue to mount in the coming years. B&J is now being challenged to find creative responses that maintain the integrity of its social, product, and economic missions.

Rational Pragmatic Greening: The Volvo Car Company

T he automobile industry produces about 34 million cars per year worldwide. There are more than 50,000 automobile accident deaths annually in the United States alone. Safety of drivers, passengers, and the public is a serious concern of the auto industry.

The primary environmental concerns related to automobiles are safety, air pollution, and fuel efficiency. The former deals with the human environment of cars, and the latter two with the impact of cars on the natural environment.

Automobiles affect the natural environment through air pollution, use of scarce oil, and scrap wastes. Auto exhaust emissions (carbon dioxide, carbon monoxide, and other gases) cause urban air pollution and smog. The large and increasing number of automobiles with low fuel efficiency consume enormous quantities of gasoline distilled from crude oil, a non-renewable fossil fuel. Maintenance of autos requires discarding batteries, tires, and parts, creating a solid waste problem. After their useful life (often less than 10 years), automobiles go into scrap yards. This represents a big waste of metal and other materials.

The Volvo Car Company tries to manage all these problems in a systematic and integrated way. For more than 40 years, safety has been a central feature of Volvo cars and the company's organizational philosophy. Within their class, Volvo cars are not as technologically sophisticated as Japanese cars, as luxurious as American cars, nor as performance-oriented as German cars. But their reputation for safety and quality has given Volvo a loyal customer base. Now Volvo has added environmental solutions to its strategy. Volvo is creating new environment-friendly, fuel-efficient cars and production facilities. It has adopted technologically rational solutions that are pragmatic from a business point of view.

Volvo is a large, diversified, international company, making cars, trucks, and engineering goods in 1992, it had revenues of $11.86 billion and 60,000 employees. Nearly 85 percent of its sales come from outside its home country of Sweden. It has been a very profitable company, declaring dividends each year since going public in 1935.

VOLVO FINANCIAL SUMMARY

Year	Sales	Net Income	EPS
1992	11.86	(0.47)	(6.11)
1991	11.03	0.09	1.26
1990	11.88	(0.14)	(1.87)
1989	12.99	0.68	8.81
1988	13.80	0.70	9.10

Sales and net income in $ billions
EPS=Earnings per share in $
Currency exchange rate, $1 = 7SKr

In recent years, foreign competition and global recession have adversely affected the company's financial performance. In 1992, it had a loss of $470 million. Under tremendous competitive pressure to maintain profitability, it is struggling to reestablish its competitive position by financial and organizational restructuring, improving productivity, and introducing product innovations.

Source: Unknown.

Even during this financially difficult period, however, Volvo is maintaining a strategic emphasis on environmental issues. Past safety programs serve as models for its environmental efforts.

A Tradition of Safety

Volvo's emphasis on safety draws upon Sweden's history and culture. The company started producing cars in 1927. The road and weather conditions in Sweden were very harsh. It was *necessary* to build a strong, high-quality car that would not fail. The Swedish mentality also encouraged this goal. Swedes saw safety as a key aspect of quality.

The focus on safety became a marketing asset in the 1940s. Volvo realized that there were many customers for whom safety was the primary criterion for choosing a car. The company created a new set of product designs and marketing innovations based on safety. It adopted an organizational structure in which several departments simultaneously dealt with safety. Volvo's safety philosophy has three key elements:

1. Car design and quality
2. Design of safe driving environments
3. Safety training of drivers

Since the 1950s Volvo has led the field in auto safety innovations. (See Table 9.1.) In 1960, Volvo created the Swedish Motor Vehicle Inspection Company to encourage the periodic inspection of vehicles. This gave another boost to the safety performance of cars, because faults and defects could be identified during the annual inspection.

The 1970s saw the creation of many new auto safety, fuel efficiency, and environmental regulations in the United States. Volvo continued to adapt to these new regulations by innovating new safety features in its cars.

PRAGMATIC SAFETY AND ENVIRONMENTAL MISSIONS

Volvo realizes that there are limits to making automobiles friendly to people and the environment. The automobile is a powerful machine and can be hazardous if not used with caution. It uses non-renewable fossil fuels and contributes to air pollution. It is a complex piece of machinery, requiring an equally complex manufacturing technology.

The company does not intend to eliminate all the harmful effects of automobiles at any cost. As it stated in a presentation to the 1972 U.N. Environmental Conference: "Volvo does not wish to protect the auto at any price and under all conditions. It is in Volvo's best interest that the auto is used in such a way that it does not cause environmental damage." The company sees society as having primary responsibility for developing an ecologically sustainable transportation system. But Volvo wants to make active contributions toward this goal.

TABLE 9.1

Chronology of Volvo Safety Design and Engineering Features

Safety Feature	Model Year Introduced in Sweden	Remarks
Safety glass windscreen with automatic windshield wiper	1927	
Passenger compartment safety cage	1944	Legal requirement in U.S. 1969
Laminated windshield	1944	Legal requirement in U.S. 1969
Windshield defroster	1954	Legal requirement in U.S. 1969
Windshield washers	1956	Legal requirement in U.S. 1969
Split steering column	1956	
Padded dashboard	1956	
Achorage for safety belts in front seats	1956	
One-piece three-point lap/shoulder seat belt	1959	Legal requirement in U.S. 1973
Padded instrument panel	1960	Legal requirement in U.S. 1970
Front wheel disc brakes on 122S model	1961	
The Volvo Chair on all models	1964	
Defroster in rear window	1966	
Impact absorbing body sections—front and rear	1966	
Dual-circuit braking system	1966	Legal requirement in U.S. 1968
Triangular split braking system	1966	Legal requirement in U.S. 1968
Child-proof rear door locks	1966	No legal requirement in U.S.
Four-wheel disc brakes on all 144 models	1967	
Three-point seat belts—rear outboard	1967	Legal requirement in U.S. 1990
Head restraints	1968	Legal requirement in U.S. 1969
Inertia reel belts—front	1969	Legal requirement in U.S. 1973
Inertia reel belts—rear outboard	1971	MY introduced in U.S. 1972
Warning light for seat belt	1971	Legal requirement in U.S. 1976

continued

TABLE 9.1 *CONTINUED*

Chronology of Volvo Safety Design and Engineering Features

SAFETY FEATURE	MODEL YEAR INTRODUCED IN SWEDEN	REMARKS
Collapsible steering column	1973	
Electric rear window defroster standard on all models	1973	
Side collision protection (steel-reinforced doors)	1973	
Multistage impact-absorbing steering wheel	1974	
Energy-absorbing bumpers	1974	MY introduced in U.S. 1976
Safety belt reminder audiovisual	1974	MY introduced in U.S. 1974
Warning lights—hazard	1975	
Braking system with stepped bore master cylinder	1975	
Warning lights on open door	1982	
Wide-angle rear view mirror	1982	
Fog lights—front and rear	1982	State regulated
Anti-lock brakes (A.B.S.)	1984	
Safety belt pretensioner	1986	Not required in U.S.
Supplemental Restraint System	1986	MY introduced in U.S. 1986
Three-point seat belt center rear position 700 series (accessory)	1987	
Top tether anchor	1989	
Three-point seat belts—all three rear positions in the 940 sedans	1991	MY introduced in U.S. 1991
Head restraints—all three rear positions in the 940 sedans	1991	MY introduced in U.S. 1991

Source: Volvo Cars of North America.

Volvo's environmental policy pledges to:

1. Develop and market products with superior environmental properties that meet the highest possible efficiency requirements.
2. Opt for manufacturing processes that have the least possible impact on the environment.
3. Participate actively in and conduct our own research and development in the environmental field.
4. Select environmentally compatible and recyclable materials for developing and manufacturing products, and as components.
5. Apply a total view regarding the adverse impact of our products on the environment.
6. Strive to attain a uniform, worldwide environmental standard for processes and products.

MANAGING THE ENVIRONMENTAL ISSUES OF TRANSPORTATION

The complexity of the automobile and its production processes requires an overall systemic view of safety and environmental protection. Volvo thus spreads its safety and environmental tasks throughout the organization, instead of locating them in a single department.

These tasks also extend beyond the company to include governmental agencies, consumers, and the general public. This requires integrating environmental and safety concerns not only into auto design and production, but also into driver training and education, highway construction, and traffic management. It requires dealing with environmental and safety issues within the entire transportation system of a society.

Volvo's responses to the environmental problems of the auto industry have focused on making fuel-efficient cars and reducing auto-exhaust emissions. It is also improving the environmental performance of its manufacturing operations. Here again, the company has adopted pragmatic and balanced solutions. It addresses all elements of the product life cycle, from raw materials to wastes and pollution.

Fuel Efficiency

Volvo has created a database for using a full life-cycle method to compare the environmental effects of different fuels. It is also experimenting with different internal combustion systems and methods of propulsion, which form the basis for developing flexible fuel vehicles (FFV). Volvo's prototype FFVs can run on combinations of batteries, gasoline, natural gas, and diesel.

Volvo launched a new series of high-efficiency, low-emission diesel engines for trucks. An Electronic Diesel Control (EDC) system monitors several important engine functions, automatically adjusting fuel injection to match running conditions. These engines reduce nitrous oxide emissions by 33 percent, compared to conventional engines.

The company is also working to improve the fuel efficiency of the country's overall transportation system. It built a road between Torslanda and Arendal in Göteborg. This, combined with a comprehensive traffic coordination program, reduced the traffic volume on the route by 1,300 vehicle-kilometers per day.

Eliminating CFCs

Volvo has a comprehensive plan to phase out the use of ozone-depleting CFCs. The Volvo 850 is already a CFC-free car. It uses plastic components foamed with HCFCs, and an R134A refrigerant, both substitutes for CFCs. Volvo's American, Swedish, and Belgian plants have stopped using halons as fire-fighting agents. The company has also discontinued the use of CFC solvents in its American and Belgian operations.

Reducing Emissions from Manufacturing

By making rational environment-oriented investments, Volvo has reduced emissions from its manufacturing plants. The Torslanda plant has shifted to using more water-based paints. This reduces the use of solvents. It uses rotary carbon filters to trap the solvents employed in conventional processes. They are incinerated in sand beds and natural-gas-fired drying ovens. The plant has cut solvent emissions 85 percent over the past decade.

Volvo redesigned its truck-painting shops in Umea, Sweden, and in Brazil to reduce paint use and purify solvent-contaminated air. At full production, the purification equipment reduces solvent emissions by 30 percent. Volvo component plants have made a major effort to reduce the use of spirit-based cutting fluids and chlorinated hydrocarbon degreasing agents.

The Skovde plant has completely stopped using these degreasing agents. It produces aluminum engines that do not need painting. Its engine test shop has fuel recovery systems. In 1991, the plant commissioned production of the largest dust collector in Scandinavia, which cuts dust emissions by half. Production plants encourage flexible manufacturing systems in order to improve productivity. They provide workers with a safer, cleaner working environment.

Chemical Inventory Reduction

Volvo's chemical inventory system attempts to reduce the use of hazardous chemicals and substitute for them substances that are environmentally friendly. In 1991, Volvo established a new database known as MOTIV, for monitoring chemical inventories. It monitors the chemicals used in each facility. It also identifies their effects on internal and external environments. Analysis and comparison of chemical use within and outside Volvo allows benign substrates to be substituted for hazardous chemicals.

Recycling and Waste Management

Automobile production generates a lot of waste. Moreover, the car itself, when discarded, is a major waste item, difficult to dispose of. Volvo's primary response to the waste issue is to design cars for durability. The average age of Volvos in use is nearly double that of American-made cars. Longer life reduces waste by reducing the number of cars scrapped each year. Volvo is also researching ways of making cars recyclable. In this area Volvo is behind BMW, which has already designed a fully recyclable car.

The Environmental Concept Car

Volvo has developed a unique product—the Volvo Environmental Concept Car (ECC). The idea behind the ECC was to create a practical, pro-environmental, fuel-efficient, and safe family car. Its design objective was to minimize the total environmental effects of production, operation, and eventual destruction. Although the car is not yet in production, its basic idea follows Volvo's tradition of combining practical technological solutions with competitive advantage.

The Volvo ECC is a hybrid car that runs on both electric motors and a gas-turbine engine. It has all the safety features and responsive power resources available in top-of-the-line Volvo cars. In city traffic it is a zero-emission vehicle because it runs on electric batteries. It can operate on all currents from 170 to 330 volts in single-phase or three-phase systems.

To minimize energy consumption, the ECC has low mass, drag, and rolling resistance. It is made of aluminum, which reduces its weight by 12 percent compared to other cars of similar size. Its aerodynamic design gives it a 30 percent lower coefficient of drag (0.23), and special tires reduce the rolling resistance by half.

The ECC uses pro-environmental materials. Its aluminum inner frame and body are recyclable. The paint on the body is water based. It uses a low-emission painting process to minimize release of hydrocarbons into the air. It uses recyclable plastics in

a design for bumper, grille, and internal panels that are easily
dismantled. It will have recyclable batteries that Volvo is now
developing.

The total environmental impact of cars may be expressed in
Environmental Load Units (ELU), a measure developed by the
Swedish Environmental Research Institute. ELU value for a car
is the sum total of ELUs for emissions, energy use, and material
consumption in the manufacture and assembly of the car,
during the car's total service life, and in the destruction or recycling of the car's components when scrapped.

Because of its hybrid nature, the ELU rating of the Volvo
ECC depends on the use of power sources during its operating
life. With the right mix (30 percent gasoline and 70 percent electrical), the ELU rating of the Volvo ECC would be as low as 30
percent of the ELU rating of today's Volvo family car. If the car
uses equal amounts of gas and electrical power, its ELU rating
would be half that of today's family cars.

MANAGING SAFETY ISSUES

Volvo's systems approach to safety is apparent in the company's
focus on safety of product, production system, and in-use car
safety. The safety system for products includes crash avoidance
engineering, an experimental safety vehicle program, crash-
worthiness engineering, and product liability and insurance
management.

Volvo designs cars to withstand *all* crash elements. The frame
and body absorb crash energy. The traction system maintains
handling characteristics in emergencies. Each year Volvo performs 70 full-scale crash tests, or 40 tests per 100,000 cars produced. In addition, it separately tests car cabins, accelerators,
and other components for safety.

Product liability management provides another way of encouraging safety. It maintains a detailed database on accidents,
and their causes and consequences. It analyses this data periodi-

cally to identify sources of failure. From this analysis emerge ideas for product improvement and driver education.

Volvo ensures production safety through careful pre-production planning and applying quality control to all stages of production. Pre-production planning may extend over five to 10 years before a car is mass-produced. During this phase, safety, performance, comfort, and other desirable attributes are integrated.

Quality-control tasks take about 10 percent of the production time. They include checking for defects, specifications, tolerances, operating characteristics in different situations, environmental factors, functional reliability, ease of maintenance, and fuel economy. Quality control gives first priority to safety and legal requirements.

Quality management extends to the subcontractors who produce 75 percent of Volvo's car parts. Volvo requires its suppliers to verify product requirements through regular inspection. One person is in charge of quality control at each stage of production. Volvo also requires suppliers to compile a quality handbook.

Another element of production safety is the safety-information feedback system. This system performs a life-cycle analysis of hazards. The average age of Volvo cars on the road is 19 years. Life-cycle analysis identifies opportunities for controlling and blocking hazards from cradle to grave. Some actions must be taken by the company during design, production, and servicing. Other actions must be taken by customers during use. Still other actions must be taken by society, by providing safety information, and infrastructure.

Volvo promotes the safety of cars in use through an extensive service network. It systematically supplies safety information to drivers, media, and the public. It evaluates feedback from customers, service centers, and the sales force. The recall committee monitors defects. Designers evaluate product features, then incorporate changes based on this feedback. If defective cars or parts are still in production, it advises plants to make changes in specifications and materials.

ORGANIZATIONAL STRUCTURE

Volvo distributes safety and environmental functions to many different parts of the company. The coordinating unit is the Safety and Environment Department, which is located in the Department of Quality. The Volvo Safety Center, part of the Product Development and Design Department, conducts crash-worthiness and crash-avoidance investigations. There is a separate Recall Committee that looks after the safety performance of cars on the road. Safety is also part of the job in production plants, marketing, service, purchasing, and public relations.

Safety and Environment Deparment

This department is in charge of the base-line safety and environmental functions required by law. It is responsible for developing policies and organization to meet regulatory requirements worldwide. It represents the company in discussions with national and international agencies on safety issues and standards. It distributes safety and environmental information to all units within the company. It compiles technical specifications needed for product liability claims and court trials. It manages approval and certification of car types.

This department also engages in liability prevention activities. These include total quality assurance, design reviews, special marketing of safety and emissions systems, legal requirements testing, and reporting on product defects. It leads the collection of internal research and external information on environmental protection issues. These include emissions and fuel economy, noise control, recycling, and scrap management.

The Volvo Safety Center

The center researches all aspects of car safety and disseminates this information throughout the company and to the public at large. Its work focuses on crash-worthiness tests and accident investigations. It feeds back findings from these investigations to product designers, vehicle drivers, and government agencies in charge of highway safety.

The Recall Committee

This independent committee, which was established in 1965, consists of specialists in production, safety, spare parts, quality, design, service, and legal issues. They monitor reports of product defects and decide on recall and remediation. Since 1965, annual deficiency reports have declined by half. The number of recalls has declined from two or three per year until 1979, to zero between 1979 and 1983, and about one per year since then, for a total of 20 recalls in just over 10 years. All recalls are voluntary and are implemented uniformly in all markets.

Safety and environmental performance have been potent competitive weapons for Volvo. In the past few years, however, many automakers have enhanced these two aspects of their cars and advertised them aggressively. With competition close on its heels, Volvo must do more than before in order to stay ahead. The company's hard-earned safety reputation suffered a setback recently. A TV commercial showed a crash scene with a Volvo car. The featured car was rigged to make its frame look stronger than it actually was.

Key Lessons of Volvo's Experience

---

1. A *pragmatic and balanced approach* to safety and environmental issues allowed the company to be a leader. It achieved

this balance by combining scientific, rational analysis with stakeholder opinions and the company's own values to develop practical solutions.

2. *Infusing safety and environmental concerns throughout the organization* is effective in making the whole organization conscious and responsive. *Organizational structure* is an important tool in this infusion.

3. Volvo draws its pragmatism and safety/environmental orientation from the deep-rooted and enduring source of *national traditions and company culture.* This strong value base makes it easy to gain employee commitment to the safety and environmental strategy.

4. A *broad conception of safety and environmental protection* allows the company to link product design, production, driver education, road conditions, traffic patterns, and waste management within its total management system. The company can thus keep track of all potential sources of safety and environmental problems.

5. Continuous *scientific research, product innovation, and rational analysis* of safety and environmental data are key ingredients of the company's pragmatic strategy.

Cost-Effective Green Technologies: The 3M Company

10

The 3M Company is the quintessential global, financially successful, diversified, innovative new products company. It is the envy of its competitors and of businesses outside its fields. It has a worldwide reputation for technological innovation and environmental responsiveness. The company develops and manufactures thousands of new products. It employs nearly 90,000 people in 52 countries. With 1992 revenues of $ 13.8 billion, it is one of the giants of American industry.

The company is among the 10 "most admired" companies in *Fortune* magazine annual surveys. It is famed for its excellent R&D and new-product innovations. Research and development expenditures in 1992 were more than $1 billion, and over the past five years were $4.3 billion. With this heavy research, the company gets at least 25 percent of its sales from products introduced within the last five years. From 1993 onward, it has raised this goal to 30 percent and four years.

3M places special emphasis on the productivity of labor, capital, and resources. Over the past five years its sales grew from $11.3 billion to $ 13.8 billion. Its net earnings went from $1.15 billion to $1.23 billion. Sales per employee went from $117,000 to $160,000. It has ambitious objectives for cost reduction and productivity improvement over the five-year period from 1990 to 1995. It aims to reduce its unit cost—in real terms—by 10 percent. This will involve reducing manufacturing cycle time by 37 percent, waste by 35 percent, and energy use by 20 percent per unit of production.

3M's FINANCIAL SUMMARY

Year	Sales	Net Income	EPS
1992	13.88	1.23	5.63
1991	13.34	1.15	5.26
1990	13.02	1.30	5.91
1989	11.99	1.24	5.60
1988	11.32	1.15	5.09
5-yr growth	5.2%	1.6%	2.5%

Sales and net income in $ billions
EPS=Earnings per share in $

3M AND GREENING

The seriousness and persistence of greening efforts at 3M make the company worthy of emulation for these achievements, too. It started focusing on environmental issues seriously in the early 1970s, long before most other companies did so. Twenty years later, it is clearly a leader in corporate environmentalism.

The phrase "cost-effective green technology" captures the central theme of the greening efforts of this company. 3M has developed many new technologies to minimize the use of natural resources, reduce pollution, and minimize and recycle wastes. It has established programs for preventing accidents and developing environmentally friendly products and packaging. Every environmental effort of the company saves significant amounts of money. For an effort to be undertaken it must show both environmental improvement and savings.

At the heart of 3M's greening is technological innovation in product design, production, and waste management. Technology is its strong suit, and the company has successfully leveraged this strength to achieve environmental conservation. It has expanded its well-known system for product innovation to include environmental innovation as well. Environmental projects are thus and integral part of the normal operating processes that encourage product innovation.

The enormous size, scope, and complexity of 3M pose special challenges to becoming environmentally responsive. The company has succeeded by having a clear vision and policies. It has moved that vision into concrete technological and administrative programs. Its 3P (Pollution Prevention Pays) program is now world-renowned.

VISION AND MISSION

Throughout the 1970s, American companies faced increased environmental regulations. The establishment of the Environmental Protection Agency and the passage of the Clean Air Act, the Clean Water Act, and many state and local pollution-related regulations forced companies to think seriously about the environmental effects of their operations. Most companies reacted by adding on conventional end-of-the-line pollution control devices.

3M realized that pollution control alone was not a satisfactory long-term solution. It was costly, and only bought time before falling short of regulatory standards. The real solution lay in *eliminating* pollution in the first place. The company's engineering excellence led it to conceive of preventing pollution through technological innovation. Innovations focused on product design, manufacturing, engineering, and research and development activities. The objectives were to comply voluntarily with and exceed regulatory standards for pollution.

In 1975, 3M initiated a conservation agenda guided by the following policies. It would:

- Solve its own environmental pollution and conservation problems.
- Prevent pollution at the source wherever and whenever possible.
- Develop products that will have a minimum effect on the environment.
- Conserve natural resources through reclamation, resource renewal, and other appropriate methods.
- Ensure that its facilities and products meet and sustain the regulations of all federal, state, and local environmental agencies.
- Assist, whenever possible, governmental agencies and other official organizations engaged in environmental activities.

The ultimate objective of these policies is to achieve zero pollution. The company supports these policies with detailed standards and guidelines in all environmental areas. For example, 3M's manual of environmental policies contains hundreds of specific policies, standards and implementation guidelines on topics such as pollution control equipment, environmental permits, above-ground tank inspections, office paper recycling, and so on.

Robert P. Bringer, vice president for Environmental Engineering and Pollution Control, captures the essence of 3M's environmental vision in the term "conservation technology." Innovative new eco-friendly technology is the main vehicle for minimizing the environmental harm caused by existing technologies.

The operational centerpiece of this conservation policy is pollution reduction through the "Pollution Prevention Pays" program. This program addresses many aspects of environmentally harmful inputs, throughputs, and outputs of the company. The main thrust, however, remains on the production system, which is the major source of pollution emissions. 3M labs and marketing organizations also established an Environmental Leadership Program for developing more products that are friendly to the environment. This program uses life-cycle analysis to minimize total life-cycle costs.

THE "POLLUTION PREVENTION PAYS" (3P) PROGRAM

The 3P program seeks to prevent pollution at source rather than removing it after it is produced. This involves product reformulation, process modification, equipment redesign, and recycling/reuse of waste materials.

In its first 15 years, from 1975 to 1989, the 3P program completed more than 2,500 pollution prevention projects. The program reduced 3M's pollution per unit of production by half. In all, it eliminated about 550,000 tons of pollutants: 123,000 tons of air pollutants, 16,400 tons of water pollutants, 409,000 tons of solid waste, and 1.6 billion gallons of wastewater. And the company saved more than $500 million.

The 3P program involves many well-defined projects. Each project must meet four criteria to receive formal recognition and funding: It must:

- Eliminate or reduce a pollutant.
- Benefit the environment through reduced energy use or more efficient use of manufacturing materials and resources.
- Demonstrate technological innovation.
- Save money through avoidance or deferral of pollution-control equipment costs, reduced operating and material expenses, or increased sales of an existing or new product.

The 3P program encourages all employees to participate. A 3P coordinating committee administers the program. The committee consists of members from 3M's engineering, manufacturing, and laboratory organizations, the corporate Environmental Engineering and Pollution Control Department, and the Industrial Hygiene Group.

In 1988, 3M extended its 3P program by adding a new $150-million investment in pollution-control devices. The objective of the 3P Plus program was to reduce all emissions 50 percent (from 1987 levels) by the year 2000. The company will return to the federal government the pollution credits that accrue to it.

A second element of the program is to accelerate research on eliminating pollution from manufacturing and products and boosting recovery and recycling of wastes. The company eliminated the use of ozone-depleting substances by 1993, well before the deadlines specified by the U.S. Environmental Protection Agency and the Montreal Protocol.

PROJECT EXAMPLES

3P projects vary widely in objectives, scope, design, and benefits. For example, a resin spray booth was producing 500,000 pounds of overspray annually. The wasted resin had to be collected, transported, and incinerated. A 3P project redesigned the spray booth and installed new spray equipment to eliminate excessive spray. The new design cost $45,000 in a one-time investment, but saves the company $125,000 every year.

Riker, 3M's pharmaceutical unit, makes a variety of medicine tablets that were coated with a solvent-solution coating. These solvents were expensive, and created pollution. Riker developed a water-based coating as a substitute for the solvent. This change eliminated the need for $180,000 in pollution-control equipment, saved $15,000 per year in materials cost, and eliminated 24 tons of air pollution a year. The changeover cost the company $60,000.

3M's Aycliffe plant in England produces face masks and respirators for industrial use. The company used to send waste from masks to landfills. The plant built an incinerator/steam-boiler combination that not only consumes the mask wastes but also produces steam to heat the plant. It cost $290,000, but generates annual savings of $170,000. The incinerator also prevents 250 tons of solid waste from going into landfills each year.

NON-POLLUTION CONSERVATION PROGRAMS

Besides its pollution elimination programs, 3M has several smaller programs aimed at energy and resource conservation. Its 20-year-old "Commute-a-Van" program uses more than 120 vans for employee ride sharing. This program has saved more than 50 million passenger miles, more than 3 million gallons of gasoline, and 1,100 tons of auto exhaust pollution.

3M's energy audits and conservation efforts cut energy use in half between 1973 and 1988, while production increased each year. Setback thermostats were installed in 3M buildings to control temperature during unoccupied hours. 3M manufacturing plants now reuse hot exhaust from combustion for product dryers and to make steam. The company made a commitment to Green Lights, an EPA-sponsored program, in which companies adopt highly efficient light technologies and facility designs.

In 1972, long before regulations mandated it, 3M decided to incinerate hazardous liquid wastes. Its Chemolite Center incinerator reduces the volume of hazardous wastes by 95 percent and toxicity by more than 99 percent. The heat recovered is used to power production facilities. To remain at the forefront of incineration technology, the equipment is regularly upgraded.

3M's packaging philosophy is to minimize materials, cost, and time of assembly. Engineers are continually developing new eco-friendly packaging to increase reuse and recycling. They have also decided to eliminate chrome and lead pigments, chlorofluorocarbons (CFCs), and polyvinylchloride (PVC) from all packaging specifications.

FROM POLLUTION PREVENTION TO ECOLOGICAL SUSTAINABILITY

The 3P program and its accomplishments are impressive by any standard. However, ironically, the riveting focus on the 3P program has made greening of 3M narrowly tied to technological solutions. The company's technocratic vision and concern for economic savings drives its environmentalism.

A technology-based approach has the drawback that risks associated with technologies are uncertain, often unknown, and changing continually. Technologies considered safe and acceptable as recently as 10 years ago may be unacceptable now or in the future. A case in point is incineration technology for dealing with wastes. 3M uses incineration technology extensively. A decade ago, experts viewed incineration as the best option for waste disposal. Today, it is coming under increasing criticism as a potentially polluting technology.

The major problem with the technocratic approach is that it de-emphasizes larger social and political questions of corporate ecological sustainability, focusing instead on small engineering problems. The question of whether the company is becoming *fundamentally* ecologically sustainable receives lesser attention.

The technocratic approach ignores or only indirectly deals with this basic issue. For example, 3M encourages resource conservation. However, it does not look at the possibility of eliminating a product line that uses scarce, nonrenewable resources. Reducing consumption of its products is also not a serious option. This would conflict with the growth goals of the company. Similarly, 3M focuses on preventing current pollution. Old inventories of wastes are not a priority.

Source: Reprinted with special permission of North America Syndicate.

Overall, 3M's technological efforts are commendable. Its limitations are largely a function of its vision, which keeps the focus on technological solutions.

LESSONS TO BE LEARNED

1. Use of *cost savings* as a criterion for choosing projects fits well with the overall logic of the firm and is a base for enduring efforts.
2. Focus on engineering solutions allows the *technological strength* of the company to be used for improving environmental performance.
3. By providing *opportunities for innovation*, and *recognition and rewards* for environmental accomplishments, the company motivates employee involvement.
4. *Top management guidance and continued support* is critical for acceptance of environmental programs.

5. Creating a separate Environmental Engineering and Pollution Control Division with an executive vice president heading it places environmental problems *on a par with other strategic programs* in the company.

II

"Green Japan, Inc."

As environmentalism sweeps across the world, Japan is preparing to capture emerging environmental markets. Japan is leveraging its pollution control experience, vast investment capacity, new technologies, and innovative organizational arrangements to develop a global environmental strategy. It stands uniquely positioned to compete in the $200-billion-a-year global environmental industry. By the year 2000, Japan hopes to produce more than $12 billion worth of pollution control, waste incineration, and water treatment equipment.

It is ironic that highly industrialized Japan, itself suffering from severe pollution and congestion, should emerge as a powerful competitor in providing environmental solutions. Japan's environmental problems and blunders are well known. For example, mercury poisoning of the Minamata Bay by effluents from the Chisso Chemical Company plant resulted in death and injury to thousands of people. The country's refusal to ban ivory products and thereby protect the African elephant has been widely criticized. It continues to use ecologically harmful dragnet fishing. It extensively uses rain forest lumber. And its urban air, rivers, and land are highly polluted.

For the past 20 years Japan has struggled to improve its internal environment. In the process, it has enacted many stringent laws, developed new technologies, and established new approaches to pollution control. It made great progress in the

1970s in cleaning up urban pollution and improving energy efficiency. By the late 1980s, its pollution and energy use per unit of GNP was lower than that of all other industrialized nations. Now "Green Japan Inc." is aggressively pulling together these experiences to market a range of pollution control technologies.

TECHNOCRATIC VISION

Japan has a technocratic vision of environmental problems and their management. The Japanese understand as well as anyone the global environmental problems caused by industrial development. However, they view technology-based industrialization as the sole option for economic growth, so their environmental efforts do not attempt to reduce industrial development.

Technological solutions focus narrowly on technological equipment, i.e., hardware. Operating procedures, worker training, and safety, and environmental policies and infrastructure are marginal parts of this vision. To Japan, pollution results from imperfect technologies, so new technologies are the solution. Environmental pollution is therefore a technological problem and a market opportunity.

Japan's strategy is to target the huge emerging market for pollution control and hazard management technologies. It is developing pollution control equipment and hardware for industries such as steel, waste incineration, wastewater treatment, treatment of flue gases, alternative energy, and automobiles. Japan is spending about $4 billion a year to broaden its already existing edge in environmental technologies over the United States and Europe.

TECHNOLOGICAL INNOVATIONS

Examples of the dramatic gains made by Japanese companies in controlling pollution are not hard to find. The Japanese steel industry is responsible for 25 percent of greenhouse gas emissions. It has slashed energy consumption per ton of steel by 20 percent since 1975. It plans to cut energy requirements by another 10 percent through the new direct iron-ore smelting process. The auto industry, led by Honda and Mitsubishi, has developed "lean burn" engines for cars that can travel up to 100 miles on a gallon of gas. The Tokyo Electric Power Company recently unveiled the highest performing electric car in existence. It can drive for 340 miles at 25 mph on a single battery, and can reach a maximum speed of 109 mph.

The market for decommissioning nuclear power plants is as huge as it is lucrative, potentially a trillion-dollar market in the coming decades. There are about 400 civilian nuclear power plants around the world, most built in the 1950s to 1970s, with a licensed useful life of about 30 years. They will need to be decommissioned in this and the next decade, and each decommissioning can cost more than $2 billion.

Japan has created a consortium of companies racing to develop a range of technologies for decommissioning these plants. These technologies include robots for cutting up a nuclear reactor core, television remote control of operations, and nuclear waste-containment vessels and disposal methods.

In the management of less hazardous wastes, such as municipal solid wastes, Japan is far ahead of the rest of the world. Its nationwide solid-waste recycling program claims to recycle 35 percent of wastes, far more than in the United States, where the figure is about 7 percent. This program involves stringent recycling laws, a strong recycling infrastructure, and a thriving government-supported market for recycled materials. The Taisei and Kajima corporations market an integrated system for sorting and transporting wastes within office buildings.

Energy resources are a critical limitation for Japan's industrial juggernaut. With funding from the powerful Ministry of International Trade and Industry (MITI), companies are developing biotechnology processes to deal with energy problems. They are attempting to extract hydrogen, the cleanest burning fuel, from air. This new process uses gene-splicing to increase the hydrogen-producing capacity of microbes and seaweed, and does not require the huge amounts of electricity that current methods demand.

Sanyo, Sharp, and Matshushita are global leaders in marketing solar batteries. Matshushita commercialized the first mercury-free alkaline battery. Fuji Electric Company is the leader in fuel-cell technology.

Air pollution control is another focus of technological innovation in Japan. Auto manufacturers are developing high-efficiency catalytic converters and fuel-efficient engines that release much less carbon dioxide than current models. Some companies are experimenting with genetically engineered microorganisms to take excess carbon dioxide out of the atmosphere.

ORGANIZATIONAL RISK SHARING

Realizing the high degree of risk in environmental business, Japan has innovated several organizational arrangements for distributing risks over many companies. They involve creative use of joint ventures with foreign firms, partnership with government agencies such as MITI, and the creation of technology consortiums.

For overseas expansion, Japanese companies have adopted joint-venture strategies. By joining with established foreign companies, Japanese firms distribute the financial risks of new projects. They also acquire industrial technologies and marketing and distribution networks.

In the pollution control market, U.S. government agencies (municipal, state, and federal) are big buyers. Having ties with U.S. companies provides competitive advantage to Japanese manufacturers. Matshushita has a joint venture with Corning, Inc., to produce chemical catalysts to remove nitrogen oxides from coal-fired plants. It has also licensed its mercury-free alkaline battery technology to U.S.-based Rayovac Corporation.

Ebara Company has signed joint ventures with Zurn Industries of Erie, Pennsylvania, and Abfall Beseitigungs Technologien of Germany to make waste incinerators.

The tradition of government–business partnership has given Japanese companies a strong competitive advantage in many industries. These include steel, consumer electronics, automobiles, and computers. Government ministries work closely with companies to study markets, design strategies, fund R&D projects, and open trade relationships. The government and corporations are targeting the environmental industry for domination in the coming decades.

MITI is funding several alternative energy resources and pollution control technologies, as mentioned above. The Office of Development Assistance (ODA), the government's development funding agency, has earmarked funds to subsidize environmental projects in Asia. MITI proposed bundling energy aid projects in China, Malaysia, and Indonesia with ODA subsidies for Japanese environmental equipment purchases. Having these powerful government agencies as allies gives Japanese companies direct entry into intergovernmental markets around the world.

A third organizational innovation used by Japanese companies is the creation of technology consortiums to generate the expensive new technologies needed for environmental management. Groups of companies in a consortium jointly fund basic research and share research results. This cuts down the time required for technological development, and reduces the financial risk for individual companies. A good example of this is nuclear power plant decommissioning technologies. The technologies involved are expensive, hazardous, and financially risky. The markets for these technologies, though definite, are in the distant future. By creating a consortium of several dozen companies to develop pieces of this technology, Japan has leapfrogged ahead of the United States.

The first nuclear power plant decommissionings in the United States and in Japan provide a contrast in approaches. General Electric's Nuclear Division has the contract to decommission a plant in Shippensburg, Pennsylvania. It is using conventional technologies to dismantle the core. Workers in nuclear-safe suits use hacksaws to cut and remove materials. The radioactive waste is removed from the plant and shipped elsewhere for storage.

The Japanese decommissioning project is serving as a test ground for new technologies under development by a consortium of firms. They are developing robotics, computers, telecommunications and materials science, as well as nuclear waste disposal technologies. These technologies will give Japan the core competencies needed to succeed in this industry over the long term.

General Electric will no doubt make more money than the Japanese companies will during their experimental phase. But the Japanese will end up with new technologies that will give them a competitive edge over the next two decades. Such long-range environmental planning is illustrated by the Tokyo Electric Power Company.

TOKYO ELECTRIC POWER COMPANY (TEPCO): TECHNO-ENVIRONMENTAL FIX

Tokyo Electric Power Company (TEPCO) is the largest private electric-utility company in the world. In 1992, it had revenues of ¥4.7 trillion, a generating capacity of 47,000 megawatts, 40,000 employees, and served about 42 million people. About 32 percent of power generated was nuclear.

By 2001, TEPCO will generate 65,000 megawatts per year, of which 42 percent will be produced by nuclear energy. This high dependence on nuclear energy creates very different environmental risks and problems for the company: risks to human health, risks that last longer and affect large geographical areas, and risks that extend to many generations and to many corporate and government institutions through nuclear plant decommissioning and nuclear-waste disposal.

TEPCO's environmental policy is to minimize the impact of its operations on the surrounding environment through technological innovations and consumption management. It seeks to balance energy production needs with environmental protection. The Plant Siting and Environmental Protection Administration, one of the five basic administrative units of the company, develops environmental programs. This unit reports directly to the president of the company. In addition, the Nuclear Power Administration unit operates a Radiological Health and Service Center. Several other departments support the environmental effort by providing help with safety, management audit, public relations, purchasing, and related functions. The Toden Educational Institute serves the important role of distributing information to stakeholders.

The central focus of TEPCO's environmental programs is on reducing pollution from current operations. (A secondary environmental focus is researching new sources of energy.) TEPCO uses advanced pollution-control technologies to minimize emissions of carbon dioxide, sulphur, and nitrous oxides, and particulates from fossil-fuel power plants. It minimizes wastewater and thermal effluents from its thermal plants.

Sulphur dioxide (SO_2) and nitrogen dioxide (NO_2) reduction measures include the use of high-quality fuels, including crude oil with low sulphur content, coal-oil mixtures, and liquid natural gas (LNG). LNG generates 32 percent of TEPCO's power. All TEPCO power plants use desulphurization equipment, flue gas denitrification technology, in-furnace NO_2 reduction systems, electrostatic precipitators, tall stacks, and particulate scrubbers. The result of these measures is impressive. Per unit of electricity generated, TEPCO emits less than 0.4 grams/kwh of SO_2 and NO_2—compared to an average of 6.5 grams/kwh SO_2 and 3.2 grams/kwh of NO_2 in the United States, Germany, the United Kingdom, and France.

TEPCO deals with water pollution by comprehensively treating all wastewater from thermal power plants, thermal effluents from thermal and nuclear plants, and turbid water from hydro plants. Technologies used include integrating condensation, precipitation, filtering, and chemical neutralization.

TEPCO uses seawater as a coolant for power plants instead of cooling tower systems. It uses thermal effluents to increase the efficiency of fish cultivation in surrounding areas. Hydro plants have turbid water treatment systems and selective discharge systems to control downstream turbidity.

TEPCO conducts environmental impact assessments for all its power plants, transmission lines, substations, and other facilities. These studies are used to get local community participation and permission for construction and for designing environmental protection and monitoring plans.

TEPCO is also exploring a range of new energy technologies that are more efficient and environmentally safer. These include high-efficiency fuel-cell technology that generates electricity through electrochemical reaction between hydrogen and oxygen. Its thermal efficiency is 43 percent, compared to the peak of 40 percent for conventional plants. In 1991, it initiated performance verification tests on an 11-megawatt water-cooled fuel-cell plant. It is developing combined cycle power generation technology with an efficiency rate of up to 48 percent. Its Integrated Coal Gasification Combined Cycle (IGCC) technology has a thermal efficiency of 43 percent.

Another method used by TEPCO to increase efficiency is load leveling. It uses standard techniques of purchasing surplus power from private producers, and rate making to match supply-and-demand patterns. It also encourages energy conservation, recovering power from waste materials, and extensive use of thermal storage devices. In 1992, it initiated 13 Electricity District Heating and Cooling Systems (DHCS). These systems use large energy-saving heat pumps to convert low-temperature exhaust heat produced by substations, sanitation plants, rivers, and sewer water into viable sources of heat. Thermal storage tanks store the heat generated by electricity at night as hot water. This heat is used to reduce demand for electricity during the day.

Projects generating natural energy from solar and geothermal sources are in various stages of experimentation. Since 1992 TEPCO has started buying back excess energy generated by solar means in households. It is testing solar batteries for use in low-voltage transmission lines. In 1993, the company's New Energy Park at the Futtsu thermal power station opened a 9-kilowatt solar power generator, and a 300-kilowatt wind generation plant.

To share risks, TEPCO cooperates nationally and internationally with many organizations to develop environmental solutions. It supports the New Energy Development Organization and the Research Institute for Innovative Earth Technologies. It has technology exchange programs with China, Taiwan, the Koreas, France, and the United States. It also has an extensive network of cooperative ventures in developing countries for alternative-energy development.

The overall thrust of TEPCO's environmental programs is on extracting higher efficiencies and controlling pollution through technological measures. The company invests extensively in these areas using conventional return-on-capital-investment (ROI) standards. Throughout the decade of the 1980s it invested more than ¥250 billion per year in environmental protection programs. These expenditures peaked at ¥320 billion in 1990. This was about 25 percent of the total capital expenditure of the company.

Both TEPCO and Japan are highly dependent on nuclear energy. They are scrambling to create an industrial infrastructure to reprocess nuclear fuels. They are experimenting with alternative technologies for disposing of low-level radioactive wastes and spent nuclear fuels. The absence of aggressive anti-nuclear and environmental movements in Japan makes environmental protection entirely a government-industry prerogative.

An overall Japanese approach to dealing with environmental problems is still evolving, and has not clearly solidified as yet. The following summary of this approach is therefore only preliminary and tentative.

ENVIRONMENTAL PROBLEM-SOLVING IN JAPAN

- Use *technological research and innovation* to develop new environmental products and solutions. Target the emerging environmental product markets as the growth markets of the coming century.
- In making *investment decisions*, take a very long-term and global view of investments in environmental technologies. By the year 2050, nearly 40 percent of world economic production will be related to energy and environmental technologies. The demand for such products will come from industrialized and developing countries. Corporate strategic planning should provide comprehensive global solutions over the long term.
- Implementation of *environmental solutions* should make financial sense. Investments in environmental protection must pass through regular financial screens for corporate investments.
- There is great potential for *cost savings* through new technologies and the conservation and reuse of energy and resources. Focusing on these savings can create lean and green corporations. A corollary to this belief is that there is no need to put the brakes on industrialization.
- Research and development *expenses and risks* can be reduced by sharing them across specially created consortiums. Government plays an important role in choosing areas for such joint investment.
- *Distribute environmental research projects widely* among companies, government institutions, universities, and international collaborative ventures. Maximize the use of specialized knowledge in these diverse institutions.

PART III

WHAT AND HOW TO GREEN

*T*his part of the book synthesizes the lessons from the case studies into tools for greening companies. Chapter 12 begins by discussing the VITO model introduced in Chapter 2. It shows how each of these elements can be greened, and includes additional corporate examples and checklists.

Chapter 13 discusses tools for greening, focusing on internal and external processes for building environmental responsiveness, which include balancing multiple trade-offs, organizational planning, conservation technologies, stakeholder communications, conflict management, and cooperative industrial ecosystem networks.

Finally, Chapter 14 offers my vision of the ecologically sustainable multinational corporation of the future. These corporations will be organized along different lines of ownership, resource exploitation, and management practices. The chapter suggests that a new communitarian capitalism is evolving, which offers many exciting economic and ecological opportunities.

From these chapters you should be able to take away ideas for action. The checklists are full of ideas that you can implement immediately.

I started this book by articulating the challenges of greening your organization. I am ending it with concrete solutions to meet those challenges. But these solutions will be effective only to the extent that *you* take personal responsibility for implementing them.

12

Greening Vision, Inputs, Throughputs, and Outputs

Traditional business management focuses on corporate profits, growth, and maximizing assets. It emphasizes economic performance. Only recently have managers begun to acknowledge the importance of ecological performance. Progressive managers are accepting responsibility for dealing with environmental issues rather than shifting them to government.

Traditional management theories need to be augmented with concepts that allow them to treat nature as a central concern for corporations. Various theories for managing organizations in continually changing environments have been proposed over the past several decades. Although they acknowledge the importance of the external environment, they do not mean the natural environment, but the economic, social, technological, commercial, and political environment.

It is time to move from Theory X, Theory Y, and Theory Z of management to an ecological theory of management, a Theory E. Theory X is the oldest and goes back to the origins of modern management thought. It espouses "scientific management." It seeks to make corporations more efficient and effective through scientific analysis of their operations. It conceives the firm to be a machine, whose performance can be optimized by managing *financial, material, and technological resources.*

Douglas McGregor's Theory Y acknowledges that corporations are more than just machines, materials, finances, and technologies. They also have living, breathing human beings who perform the tasks. Theory Y emphasizes management of *human resources*. It acknowledges the importance of human factors in achieving efficiency.

In the last decade, William Ouchi (1980) proposed a Theory Z of managing corporate *cultures and values* as powerful handles for motivating and eliciting better performance from employees.

The fundamental purpose of corporations now needs to go beyond technical/financial/human performance to include ecological performance. Corporations need to seek efficiencies for minimizing impacts on the environment. They need to acknowledge the central importance of the natural environment, and to consider the relationships of organizations to nature in making strategic decisions.

An Ecological Approach to Management

We need an expanded theory of management that builds on past theories, based on the assumption that economics interacts with ecology and that virtually every aspect of a company has some impact on its natural and human environments. Let us call it "Theory E." It focuses on managing corporations as if the *Earth (ecology)* really mattered, and includes the preservation and enhancement of our natural and human environments among the central purposes of corporations.

The experiences of the companies discussed in previous chapters suggest at least four key elements of a Theory E. All these companies were able to achieve exemplary environmental performance through *integrated greening of vision, inputs, throughputs, and outputs.*

Corporations represent a group of people working toward common goals. People unite in order to achieve a common *vision* of a mutually beneficial future. This vision determines the company's missions, goals, and values. It expresses the company's relationship with its members, its stakeholders, the community, and its natural environment.

To achieve their goals, companies create a system of inputs, throughputs, and outputs. *Inputs* include human efforts, finances, physical raw materials, and energy—all necessary to make products and services. These inputs come from finite stocks of human and natural resources. The system of *throughputs* consists of manufacturing, warehouse, and transportation facilities, often involving polluting emissions, hazardous work environments, and risky distribution systems. *Outputs* include products and wastes that pose environmental and safety problems.

These organizational elements also correspond to the life-cycle of products and businesses. Analysis of the environmental consequences of these elements is the essence of life-cycle analysis, a popular technique for environmental management.

These four elements of corporations directly affect the natural environment, so any true greening of companies must address all of them; it cannot be a partial effort, focusing on one or a few elements. It cannot be a superficial public relations response to public environmental concerns, nor can it be an isolated response to one urgent environmental problem. True greening demands total transformation of a corporation's basic values and missions, inputs, throughputs, and outputs throughout the entire product life-cycle.

CORPORATE VISION AND THE ENVIRONMENT

The "vision" of any corporation is a broad term representing the values, beliefs, missions, philosophy, and culture that together guide its activities. It reflects a corporation's fundamental assumptions about itself, the very foundations on which it stands.

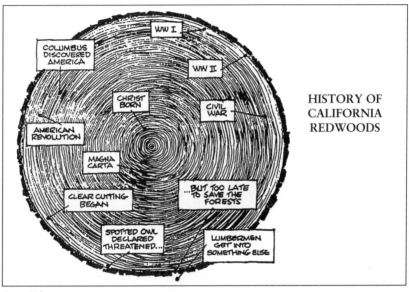

HISTORY OF
CALIFORNIA
REDWOODS

Source: Unknown.

Corporate vision can limit the company's activities to technological, market, and financial matters, or it can expand them to
include social, ecological, and human concerns. It can define a
company's relationship with nature as one-way exploitation of
resources or a mutually beneficial interdependent relationship.

If concern for nature is absent from a company's vision, it
will also be absent from other organizational elements—
products, strategies, policies, programs, recruitment and training, resource allocation, technologies, and systems. Because of
these extensive implications, greening of corporate vision must
be in place before complete corporate greening can be possible.

To see how vision affects all other aspects of a company, consider the following statement by AT&T:

> We believe environmental protection is not only a social
> issue but a business imperative. It's our view that industry-
> related environmental problems are the result of operating
> defects that can be remedied through better quality man-
> agement and new technology.

Implicit in this view are solutions to environmental problems that AT&T is pursuing. The company is not simply catching waste at the end of a run-off pipe, or adding scrubbers to a smokestack. It is developing a range of programs to get at the root cause of environmental problems. It is changing the production system to deliver higher environmental performance.

AT&T cut back the use of CFCs by 60 percent by 1991. By using new manufacturing technology and procedures, it eliminated CFCs altogether by 1994, a year ahead of the national goal. These technologies eliminated CFC-based cleaning solvents, or substituted for it other cleaners, including one made from an extract of orange peels. In some cases, operating changes eliminated the need to clean circuit boards.

AT&T cut toxic air emissions by 68 percent in 1991, and plans to eliminate them by the year 2000. To cut air pollution and save gasoline, it is experimenting with telecommuting so that employees can work from home. Its solid-waste-management program led to recycling 44 million pounds of paper in 1990. By 1994, it reduced manufacturing waste by 25 percent, reduced paper use by 15 percent, and recycled 35 percent of the paper it does use.

A green vision acknowledges the importance of the natural and human environments of a company. It offers the company a non-traditional view of its missions, goals, growth, profits and organizational well-being. A green vision sees profits as necessary but not sufficient for corporate survival and competitiveness. A green vision seeks ecological, international, competitive, and ethical sustainability. In carrying out such a vision, corporate and competitive strategies play a central role.

To create a green vision, managers may adopt the "Business Charter for Sustainable Development" presented in Chapter 2. Alternatively, managers may adapt the guidelines proposed by the Coalition for Environmentally Responsible Economies (CERES).

The CERES Principles
(FORMERLY THE VALDEZ PRINCIPLES)

INTRODUCTION

By adopting these Principles, we publicly affirm our belief that corporations have a responsibility for the environment, and must conduct all aspects of their business as responsible stewards of the environment by operating in a manner that protects the Earth. We believe that corporations must not compromise the ability of future generations to sustain themselves.

We will update our practices constantly in light of advances in technology and new understandings in health and environmental science. In collaboration with CERES, we will promote a dynamic process to ensure that the Principles are interpreted in a way that accommodates changing technologies and environmental realities. We intend to make consistent, measurable progress in implementing these Principles and to apply them to all aspects of our operations throughout the world.

PROTECTION OF THE BIOSPHERE

We will reduce and make continual progress toward eliminating the release of any substance that may cause environmental damage to the air, water, or the Earth or its inhabitants. We will safeguard all habitats affected by our operations and will protect open spaces and wilderness, while preserving biodiversity.

SUSTAINABLE USE OF NATURAL RESOURCES

We will make sustainable use of renewable natural resources, such as water, soils, and forests. We will conserve nonrenewable natural resources through efficient use and careful planning.

continued

REDUCTION AND DISPOSAL OF WASTE

We will reduce and where possible eliminate waste through source reduction and recycling. All waste will be handled and disposed of through safe and responsible methods.

ENERGY CONSERVATION

We will conserve energy and improve the energy efficiency of our internal operations and of the goods and services we sell. We will make every effort to use environmentally safe and sustainable energy sources.

RISK REDUCTION

We will strive to minimize the environmental, health, and safety risks to our employees and the communities in which we operate through safe technologies, facilities, and operating procedures, and by being prepared for emergencies.

SAFE PRODUCTS AND SERVICES

We will reduce and where possible eliminate the use, manufacture, or sale of products and services that cause environmental damage or health or safety hazards. We will inform our customers of the environmental impacts of our products or services and try to correct unsafe use.

ENVIRONMENTAL RESTORATION

We will promptly and responsibly correct conditions we have caused that endanger health, safety, or the environment. To the extent feasible, we will redress injuries we have caused to persons or damage we have caused to the environment and will restore the environment.

INFORMING THE PUBLIC

We will inform in a timely manner everyone who may be affected by conditions caused by our company that might endanger health, safety, or the environment. We will regularly seek advice and counsel through dialogue with persons in communities near our facilities. We will not take any action against employees for reporting dangerous incidents or conditions to management or to appropriate authorities.

MANAGEMENT COMMITMENT

We will implement these Principles and sustain a process that ensures that the Board of Directors and Chief Executive Officer are fully informed about pertinent environmental issues and are fully responsible for environmental policy. In selecting our Board of Directors, we will consider demonstrated environmental commitment as a factor.

AUDITS AND REPORTS

We will conduct an annual self-evaluation of our progress in implementing these Principles. We will support the timely creation of generally accepted environmental audit procedures. We will annually complete the CERES Report, which will be made available to the public.

DISCLAIMER

These Principles establish an environmental ethic with criteria by which investors and others can assess the environmental performance of companies. Companies that sign these Principles pledge to go voluntarily beyond the requirements of the law. These Principles are not intended to create new legal liabilities, expand existing rights or obligations, waive legal defenses, or otherwise affect the legal position of any signatory company, and are not intended to be used against a signatory in any legal proceeding, for any purpose.

This amended version of the CERES Principles was adopted by the CERES Board of Directors on April 18, 1992.

GREENING CORPORATE AND COMPETITIVE STRATEGIES

Corporate strategies describe who the company is and what it wants to be in the future. They define the corporation's philosophy, goals, and products and describe its domain of operation. They show what the company plans to do in the future.

Competitive strategies make individual business units competitive within their industry. They describe how a particular business will produce, price, promote, and distribute its products to its customers. They are the source of sustainable competitive advantage.

Historically, strategic planning has focused on market and financial considerations. It has sought to ensure that the corporation operates in attractive markets that have steady demand, are growing, provide good returns and shield the company from volatility. Financially, it emphasizes the importance of continuous growth, profitability, and increasing stockholder wealth.

Nowhere in this process is any attention given to how products and production systems relate to the *natural environment.* But all strategic aspects of corporations have environmental consequences. This offers a powerful new focus for designing corporate and competitive strategies. Each strategy can be given an environmental twist.

Formulating environmentally sensitive strategies requires examining the relationships between traditional market and financial considerations, and environmental ones. The popular myth is that environmental considerations invariably conflict with market and financial objectives. The examples of companies cited in this book disprove this myth.

Sustainable green strategies explicitly position the firm in relation to its natural environment. Products and business-portfolio choices consider the relationship of product, packaging, and production systems to safety, health, and environmental concerns. These choices seek to conserve resources and energy, improve production efficiency, and minimize pollution and waste. The potential for green strategies exists in nearly all industrial and technological sectors.

For example, The Body Shop created green strategies in the cosmetics industry, whose products consist predominantly of synthetic chemicals. In contrast, The Body Shop sells only natural, safe, minimally packaged products that are not tested on animals. Through its strategies, the company shows that it really cares about its customers' health and about the natural environment. The company has created a unique identity through this strategy. It has attracted committed international vendors and franchisees who share its vision and values. They are a source of sustainable competitive advantage against larger competitors.

Another company pursuing green strategies in a traditionally polluting industry is Green Bay Packaging, Inc. This company produces a variety of recycled-paper and container-board products in ecologically sound production facilities. It developed three new container boards used to manufacture corrugated boxes. Eco-brite and Eco-white container boards have a surface of recycled newspapers or recycled white paper, and use 50 percent recycled corrugated materials. Eco-stack container board uses 100 percent recycled high-performance container board and is up to 20 percent lighter than regular container boards.

Green Bay's timber conservation and waste-paper recycling practices go back to 1956, when the company innovated processes to convert formerly burned waste products and waste paper into recycled paper and cardboard. It was also the first company to develop and commercialize a non-polluting method for burning spent sulfite coking chemicals, and to recycle process water. It is known for its solid-waste recycling and design of pollution-abatement pulp and paper machinery. Thus, it is a green company, even in a highly polluting and environmentally destructive industry.

The essence of green strategies lies in realizing "ecological efficiencies." These are savings in materials, manufacturing costs, design, human efforts, transportation, and storage that si-multaneously benefit the ecology. Eco-efficiencies are a vast, un-tapped source of productivity.

GREENING INPUTS

Corporations use a variety of inputs to manufacture products and services, including energy, raw materials, plant and equip-ment, human labor, and finances. Inputs also include administra-tive, maintenance, logistical, and transportation systems that support corporate activities. Working with vendors who supply them, companies can change the ecological effects of these in-puts. (See checklist.)

Raw Materials and Energy

The biggest eco-efficiency potential lies in the conservation of raw materials and energy. In the past companies simply did not exploit such efficiencies. They assumed that basic resources such as water and air would always be available abundantly at nom-inal prices. Now companies are realizing the high costs of main-taining the desired quality of these resources. These costs point to the need for improving ecological performance.

Directly or indirectly, inputs have consequences for the envi-ronment. Some industries make heavy use of natural raw mate-rials, such as coal and oil, forest products, agricultural products, marine products, and minerals. They extract these resources and diminish the amount available.

The ecological and social devastation caused by rapacious mining is evident across the United States in the abandoned open-pit coal mines of central Pennsylvania and in the copper-mine tailings that sully the rivers of Colorado. The physical blight on the environment is coupled with the plight of the dying communities that depended on these resources.

Even companies that are not extracting natural raw materials make extensive use of natural resources. They use land for lo-

GREENING VENDORS CHECKLIST

☑ Develop a policy on environmental performance of raw materials, sub-assemblies, components, consumables, etc., consistent with your company's environmental policy and mission statements. Circulate the policy to all vendors.

☑ Establish a vendor management program with benchmarks for achieving specific targets for implementing the policy. Share the written policy with vendors. Make presentations to key vendors. Establish specific responsibility for greening of each vendor.

☑ Identify cost savings, regulatory requirements, PR benefits, competitive advantages of environmentally sound supplies. Use this to convince your own buyers and vendors to become ecologically responsible.

☑ Get vendors involved in discussion of environmentally sound substitute materials, production techniques, packaging, storage systems, and inventory management.

☑ Pool your purchasing power. Work in cooperation with other buyers and your industry trade association to create a large buying consortium. As a group you can insist on more ecologically sound supplies.

☑ Reward and encourage environmentally responsible vendors with longer time contracts and better terms.

☑ Share the risk of developing new environmentally sound products with your vendors. For selected items that require research and development investment, you can guarantee a certain quantity of annual purchases.

☑ Periodically assess vendors' environmental performance in relation to your own company's environmental performance. Vendors that are falling behind should be urged to improve their performance. Do not expect vendors to do things your own company is not doing.

cating facilities, as landfill space, for burying toxic wastes, and for housing employees. They use water in production processes for cooling, cleaning, diluting, and storing. They use rivers and seas as sinks for discharging wastes.

Enormous potential exists for reducing the environmental impact of this consumption. For example, in the energy sector, millions of dollars can be saved simply through conservation. In 1991, $2 billion was invested in 1,300 energy conservation programs in 200 utility companies across the United States. By the year 2000, conservation efforts will save the equivalent of the energy produced by 24 large power plants. Studies by Amory Lovins show that electricity from new power plants costs about 10 cents per kilowatt-hour to generate. In contrast, conservation programs cost about five cents (some programs cost less than one cent) per kilowatt-hour saved. And the potential is there to conserve 50 percent to 75 percent of the current amount of energy used.

With such attractive economics, energy conservation holds the largest potential for greening of corporations. Moreover, simple conservation through innovations in architecture and lighting offer big savings. The new National Audubon Society headquarters building in New York City was designed to use 68 percent less energy than is required by conventional building designs. In its co-generation program, the Pennsylvania Power & Light Company uses wastes to generate electricity. The waste steam heats a greenhouse. (See checklist.)

Substitution of raw materials also holds great potential for ecological efficiencies. Input resources must be managed in a way that prevents their depletion. This can be achieved by pacing their use, allowing them to regenerate themselves naturally. The checklist on page 187 provides some suggestions for material recycling and renewal.

Plastic, a derivative of petroleum, is the most widely used and the most widely discarded material in the world. General Electric and Dupont are conserving virgin plastic resin by encouraging the use of recycled plastics. Herman Miller, the furniture manufacturer, successfully replaced old hardwoods from endangered forests in making of furniture. Newspaper companies are

---

GREENING ENERGY USE CHECKLIST

☑ Conduct a comprehensive energy audit to identify heat and electric-load distribution and opportunities for conservation. Free audit services are often available from local electrical equipment vendors, town engineers, and utility companies.

☑ Install energy-efficient equipment such as temperature regulators, automatic off switches, and insulation, and as replacements for old motors, compressors, heaters, coolers, control devices, and office equipment. In most cases these investments have reasonable payback periods.

☑ Generate your own electricity from waste, solar, or wind energy sources.

☑ Join EPA's Greenlights Program (telephone 202-382-4992) to replace conventional light bulbs with more efficient fluorescent alternatives.

☑ Install heat recovery and storage systems where economically feasible.

☑ Use waste heat from neighboring facilities to meet your heating load if it is available.

☑ Use energy-efficient building designs for new buildings. Consider earth-sheltered spaces.

☑ Encourage and reward energy-efficient behavior, such as switching off lights, computers, and equipment when not needed.

☑ Use solar energy power whenever possible, such as for late-night outside lighting, desk-top calculators, and certain types of heating applications.

---

saving millions of dollars each year by using recycled newsprint paper, saving precious trees.

Forest product companies are switching to sustainable yield forestry to ensure a continued supply of dwindling forest resources.

GREENING PAPER USE CHECKLIST

☑ Cut back on the use of paper by establishing an office electronic mail system and using communications networks.

☑ Cut back on use of paper by being brief, limiting communications to one page whenever possible, using summaries instead of full reports, and reducing the number of rough drafts printed.

☑ Maximize the use of each page by reducing margins, using one and a half instead of double spacing, using a smaller typeface, using half and quarter pages instead of a full page.

☑ Eliminate forms. Critically question all the standard forms used in routine operations. Reduce the number of copies.

☑ Control photocopying. Urge employees to avoid making extra copies.

☑ Encourage reuse of paper by using back side of paper for memos and rough work, selling paper for use as farm-animal bedding, etc.

☑ Minimize mass mailings by using voice-mail systems, posting notices at frequently used public areas. Share copies of reports, notices, memos within departments instead of distributing to individuals.

☑ Establish a paper recycling program that covers all types of papers and paper boards.

☑ Stop thinking of paper as paper, and think of it as trees. Plant enough trees to replace the paper used annually by your company.

Human Resources

People are a basic ingredient for greening. Unless companies can convince and motivate their employees, environmental initiatives will not take root. It is important to recruit, train, promote, and reward employees for environmental performance.

The key to greening employees is empowering them to take up environmental initiatives. *Empowerment* means creating an organizational culture and processes by which workers themselves can articulate ideas, develop them into programs, and im-

GREENING MATERIAL USE—RECYCLING AND RESOURCE RENEWAL CHECKLIST

☑ Conduct a comprehensive materials audit. Identify scarce and ecologically risky materials in use and seek substitutes for them.

☑ Conduct an environmental impact analysis for major raw materials. Identify and rectify any environmental damage that use of these materials is causing.

☑ Establish recovery and recycling programs for all major materials, including oils, paper, metals, glass, plastics, acids, solvents, water, etc.

☑ Develop an integrated waste-management program that makes judicious use of reuse, recycling, incineration, composting, and landfilling.

☑ Eliminate or reduce the use of hazardous materials. Many hazardous materials common in past years have safer substitutes today. Use zinc coatings instead of cadmium, CFC substitutes, PCB-free transformers, asbestos-free brake linings, low-sulphur coals, unleaded gasoline, etc. If elimination is not feasible, store hazardous materials in small quantities instead of in bulk.

☑ Establish hazardous materials emergency and spill recovery plans. Communicate the plans to surrounding communities.

☑ Establish inventory management systems that minimize material losses, spoilage, in-transit waste. Experiment with just-in-time inventory systems.

☑ Consider resource-renewal programs for replacing the resources used by the company: plant trees, create compost from wastes, generate energy from renewable sources.

plement them. The best ideas are likely to originate at the operating level—on shop floors, in warehouses, at service centers, in sales and service areas. People doing daily tasks are in the best position to assess the environmental effects of their work. They understand what they are doing and know what can be changed to improve the work's environmental impact.

GREENING THROUGHPUTS

A *throughput system* represents all the activities involved in converting inputs into outputs: the production system, warehouse facilities, transportation systems, logistical support services, and the administrative infrastructure of the company.

Production Systems

The first step in greening a throughput system is to improve its technological operating efficiency—improve the material and energy productivity of the production system. This can be achieved through improved designs to stop losses, leakages, and waste, proper maintenance of plant and equipment, reducing duplication and redundancies, and eliminating pollution. Ultra-high-efficiency, zero-pollution factories are now being planned by many companies, including AT&T, 3M, and Dupont.

Organization

Companies that have institutionalized environmental management have supportive organizational systems and structures. First, top managers act as champions of the environmental cause, and publicly declare their support for environmental programs. They provide encouragement and political and material support for environmental actions.

Companies use the support of top managers to elicit support from the rest of the organization. At The Body Shop and Ben & Jerry's, the CEOs have been outspoken about environmentalism. They serve as the lightning rods for environmental actions. Some companies, such as Union Carbide and Du Pont, have established board committees to oversee environmental performance. Others, such as Dow Chemical, have created corporate environmental councils made up of diverse stakeholder groups. These high-level committees provide advice and policy ideas directly to top management. They also monitor the environmental performance of the company.

A second attribute of green companies is that they have explicit corporate environmental policies describing environmental goals, action plans, and resource allocations. They act as a general blueprint for action, providing the systems and procedures needed.

A third feature is that they have clearly allocated the responsibilities for where policy is formed and where it is put into action. Forming environmental policy and monitoring and evaluating performance occur at headquarters. But implementing policy is the responsibility of business units and operating plants. In implementing policies, operating-unit managers custom tailor them to their local conditions.

A fourth, key element of successful environmental management is empowering and energizing employees or workers. Sound environmental management involves allowing ordinary workers to bring out, assess, and develop their ideas. (See the checklist on greening employees on page 190.)

In such situations people feel that they have influence and seem to have fun doing environmental projects. Ben & Jerry's "green teams" and the informal, uninhibited environment at The Body Shop are examples.

SHE POLICIES AND PROGRAMS

Policies dealing with safety, health, and the environment (SHE policies) are commonplace in today's corporations. The law requires them. They provide employees with much-needed information and guidance. The focus here is not on describing the policies, but on how to improve them.

The McDonald's Corporation's waste reduction policy is a good example of a well-conceptualized environmental policy. Developed in conjunction with the Environmental Defense Fund, it also serves as an excellent example of partnership between business and environmental groups.

McDonald's owns 25 percent of its 8,500 restaurants and franchises the remainder. It has 600 suppliers. It generates 238

GREENING EMPLOYEES CHECKLIST

☑ Extend your company's green mission statement and environmental policies to cover recruitment, training, work climate, culture, employment contracts, personnel benefits, and other human resource policies.

☑ Encourage maximum involvement of employees in environmental programs. Begin with small efforts, such as recycling, energy conservation, waste reduction, etc.

☑ Create an open communications process by which employee ideas for environmental projects can be collected, evaluated, and implemented.

☑ Train/educate employees to identify the connections between their jobs and ecological issues. Use external environmental training seminars to help employees build networks with outside experts and business associates.

☑ Empower lower-level workers to initiate environmental efforts in their respective areas of responsibility. Make environmentalism a grassroots effort in the company.

☑ Use committed individuals as program champions to lead environmental efforts, even if they are not heads of departments.

☑ Use employment contracts and job descriptions to establish environmental performance expectations from employees.

☑ Establish monetary rewards and public recognition for exemplary environmental initiatives. Use symbolic rewards and ceremonial recognition to build enthusiasm for environmental efforts.

☑ Get the CEO and other top management explicitly to support environmental programs. Broadcast the message of this support widely and repeat it periodically.

☑ Encourage employees to do environmentally oriented projects in the communities in which the company operates. Encourage community tie-ups, community-based environmental campaigns, enhanced community presence.

lbs/day/restaurant of on-premises waste or 0.12 lb per customer served, 80 percent of which is behind-the-counter waste.

Perseco, McDonald's package subsidiary, generates 149 lbs/day/restaurant of primary packaging. This consists of paperboard, molded pulp, paper, polystyrene, and polyethylene. Of this, 80 percent is paper and 15 percent is polystyrene.

This waste is not only a burden on landfills, it also represents wood and energy consumed for the paper and ozone-destroying CFCs for the polystyrene.

McDonald's initiated its policy in April 1991, and by 1993 was using a judicious combination of source reduction, reuse, recycling and composting to deal with 80 percent of the solid waste generated by all 8,500 restaurants.

In 1991, McDonald's established an annual evaluation procedure to identify opportunities to reduce waste at the source. It replaced polystyrene clamshells with paper-based wraps. It substituted unbleached paper for bleached paper in carryout bags, and introduced unbleached Big Mac wrap. It converted to oxygen-bleached coffee filters.

To increase reuse of materials, McDonald's replaced heavy-duty, plastic-lined corrugated boxes with durable, washable containers for delivering meat and poultry to restaurants. It replaced short-lived wooden shipping pallets with reusable durable pallets in distribution centers. It replaced single-portion packages of cleaning supplies with bulk packaging. It is pilot-testing reusable over-the-counter dishware, ketchup containers, coffee filters, and bulk-quantity condiment dispensers.

McDonald's recycles everything it can, consistent with local and regional hauling, recycling, and composting services. It is developing its own collection programs and encouraging entrepreneurs to provide such services. Its packaging currently consists of 29 percent recycled materials. The company will buy $100 million worth of post-consumer materials each year.

McDonald's has also initiated composting in the fast-food industry. It established a testing program to identify the separation, collection, and processing requirements of restaurant waste.

McDonald's realizes that to be effective, it must establish accountability within the company and partnerships with suppliers. To instill environmental commitment, it incorporates waste-reduction goals into packaging specifications, job descriptions, and decision-making processes. Suppliers and distribution centers are evaluated by these goals. The company holds annual environmental conferences for suppliers and annual waste-characterization studies to establish waste-reduction goals for the next year.

This comprehensive policy has changed McDonald's fundamental orientation and commitment to the environment. It is affecting the way the entire company and its employees treat environmental concerns. It is slowly transforming the company's culture.

Companies can also create *new* policies in innovative areas of special expertise to address larger environmental problems. For example, IBM uses computers for environmental preservation work. IBM Scientific Centers around the world work with local scientific organizations to develop solutions to local ecological problems.

In Kuwait, the IBM Scientific Center works with the Kuwait Institute of Scientific Research on spotting oil slicks from the air. By shining laser beams on water waves, scientists obtain a "fingerprint" of the spilled oil. They compare it with their database of more than 200 oil samples from the Persian Gulf to identify the source of the spill.

The IBM Scientific Center in Rio de Janeiro is working with Electronorte, a large Brazilian electric utility. They are processing Landsat satellite images with computers to identify changes in forested, planted, and urban areas over long time periods.

IBM Denmark is working with the University of Denmark and Danish Hydrolic Institute to develop an expert system that will help keep untreated water from reaching the land or sea.

There are several lessons that others can learn from the policy experiences of green companies.

First, companies must ensure that policies cover all relevant SHE functions. The law often requires coverage only of key sources of risk. But companies can go beyond compliance to create policies that aid their employees in minimizing risks to lowest possible levels.

Second, companies should ensure worldwide application of SHE policies and standards. Having policies on paper is not enough. They must produce results, and these results should be measured and rewarded.

Measuring environmental performance reliably is not easy. Measures useful for tracking SHE performance include the GEMI environmental sustainability index, reportable emissions, hazard inventories, number of accidents, and annual person/days lost to injuries.

Pollution Prevention and Control

Polluting emissions are a chronic problem of the throughput system, particularly in manufacturing and energy production. Power and chemical plants are major sources of air pollution. Fossil fuel power plants emit large amounts of sulphur dioxide and nitrous oxides, and chemical plants release chemicals from their production facilities.

The only successful way of dealing with pollution is to prevent it in the first place, because trying to clean up pollution after it is produced is not very effective. Numerous companies such as Amoco, Chevron, Dow, and 3M have reduced their chemical emissions by 50 to 90 percent over the past five years.

There are several reasons why this has been possible. First, pollution emissions depend in part on the age of plants. Older plants, especially those on which maintenance has been deferred, tend to have rusty and leaky pipes with unreliable joints, less efficient furnaces, and poor insulation. By repairing and refurbishing these old plants, a large number of small emissions can be eliminated.

Second, new plant designs offer the opportunity to eliminate or drastically reduce polluting processes. The idea of "closed loop" manufacturing eliminates discharges altogether. IBM and AT&T are both designing plants with zero emissions. Dow Chemical's ethylene plant in Fort Saskatchewan will release only 10 gallons of cleaned-up wastewater per minute, as opposed to 360 gallons for similar plants.

Third are pollution control technologies. In the past decade, these technologies have advanced tremendously in many industries. The most polluting industries, such as those producing chemicals, pulp and paper, and electric power, and refining oil, have made the most impressive advances.

GREENING OUTPUTS

Product and Production Design

Product and packaging design has great potential for improving the safety, health, and environmental performance of companies. Design for the Environment (DFE) focuses on the design of products and production technologies. By designing environmental and safety performance into their products, companies can cut environmental liabilities at the source.

Traditional design approaches use function, cost, and technical efficiency as primary design criteria. They also incorporate ease of maintenance, availability of materials, and operator convenience. DFE emphasizes environmental criteria. Choices are based on environmental and health effects, product disposal, hazard characteristics, risk levels, and safety. DFE also focuses on the product's interaction with humans, its natural environ-

GREENING PHYSICAL FACILITIES CHECKLIST

☑ Retrofit insides of buildings to save energy and minimize hazardous materials to provide healthy work spaces.

☑ Retrofit outsides of buildings to respect the natural landscape. Design the landscape not just for beauty, but also for natural integrity, energy efficiency, low maintenance, and green public spaces.

☑ Minimize the use of agrochemicals, pesticides, and fertilizers by using indigenous plants and grasses, and integrated pest management systems.

☑ Build bicycle paths on office land to encourage use of bicycles.

☑ Change land use to improve productivity. Grow food on vacant land and roof tops, create usable green spaces for employee and community use, plant trees and vines around buildings to reduce energy needs.

☑ Do an environmental audit of all corporate land to identify and clean up contaminated property. Identify and address natural hazards such as flood plains, radon gas, geological faults, and soil and drainage problems.

☑ Establish on-site and off-site plans for environmental emergencies and crises. Rehearse these plans with local police, community, hospitals, and other service agencies.

☑ Choose ecologically sound sites for locating facilities. In addition to complying with land zoning regulations, consider proximity to hazardous facilities, transportation costs, and the environmental history of the site.

☑ Establish nature conservation programs by sponsoring tree plantings, and by preserving wetlands, marshes, and other special geological features.

ment, and its organizational context, and attempts to design it for disassembly and recycling.

There are dramatic examples of the potential of DFE to eliminate major environmental catastrophes. Both the *Exxon Valdez* and Bhopal disasters involved design errors. DFE would have urged a double-hull design for the *Exxon Valdez*, reducing chances of a spill in an accident. In Bhopal, DFE would have recommended MIC (methyl isocyanate) storage in small barrels instead of huge 45-ton tanks. In small barrels, a large runaway reaction would not be possible.

Procter & Gamble, among other consumer products companies, is making innovative packaging changes that result in environmentally friendly products. Its laundry detergent Tide, once sold in liquid form, is now available in dehydrated powder form. Customers can mix it with water at home to make it liquid.

The environmental savings from this simple change are enormous. It eliminates a great many plastic bottles going to landfills. It saves transportation costs, because dehydrated powder weighs one-tenth of the liquid version of the detergent. And it saves processing water.

The important thing to note here is that the costs of these changes are minor, and customers have responded positively to such changes.

In the automobile industry, new engine designs hold great potential for pollution control and energy conservation. Honda and Mitsubishi have developed a "lean-burn" automobile engine rated at 100 miles per gallon that reduces exhaust waste. GM's Impulse electric car runs on 32 10-volt batteries. It weighs just 2,200 pounds, uses no fossil fuel, and produces zero discharge. Cars using compressed natural gas produce 80 percent less carbon monoxide and ozone-depleting gases but have the same operating costs as gasoline-burning cars.

The greening transportation checklist provides some useful suggestions for how companies can reduce the environmental effects of their own modes of transportation.

Waste Reduction, Recycling, Disposal

Waste is a major environmental hazard emanating from industry. Both solid wastes and toxic wastes pose daunting envi-

---

GREENING TRANSPORTATION CHECKLIST

☑ Reduce unnecessary transportation by re-examining need for travel, coordinating events, using courier or mail services, using e-mail, encouraging employees to live close to work locations, and purchasing supplies locally. Use a travel expert to do a travel-needs assessment.

☑ Improve the fuel efficiency of your transportation fleet by regular maintenance of vehicles, limited-speed driving, and driver-efficiency training.

☑ Establish a car-pool program. Provide economic incentives for employees to use car pools.

☑ Establish transportation pollution control measures, such as use of unleaded fuel, recycling of engine oil and air-conditioner CFCs, safe disposal of antifreeze and other consumables.

☑ Experiment with alternative fuel vehicles for specific transportation needs, such as electric delivery trucks, electric fork lifts, multiple fuel cars, bicycles or motor scooters for personal movement on office campuses, etc.

☑ Support efficient mass transportation systems in the community. Encourage employees to use the system by subsidizing parking at transit points, giving rebates to employees for using public transportation, and providing free shuttles to and from public transit stations.

---

ronmental problems. Solid waste created by households and industry goes into landfills. Within five years there will be no more landfill space. Toxic wastes are buried across the country in more than 35,000 sites. Many of these sites are active health hazards.

Controlling wastes is an unavoidable business imperative. A three-pronged approach to waste management popularized by the EPA is now widely accepted:

1. Wastes must be reduced at their source through product and process-design changes.
2. Ways must be found to reuse and recycle wastes. The United States produces more than 25 percent of the world's solid

waste but recycles less than 7 percent, compared to 35 to 40 percent in Japan.

3. Waste that cannot be eliminated or recycled must be disposed of appropriately.

There are some excellent waste-management programs that can serve as models for corporate effort. 3M Company's "Pollution Prevention Pays" program, described earlier, is a classic. It reduces pollution at the source through product reformulation, process modification, equipment redesign, and recycling and reuse. From 1975 to 1989 it has, as noted, saved the company more than $500 million and prevented 500,000 tons of pollution.

Chevron initiated its "Save Money and Reduce Toxics" (SMART) program in 1986. The EPA cited this program as one of the top 10 waste and pollution management programs in the country. Chevron succeeded in reducing waste, cutting air emissions, and reducing water pollution by 50 percent. It reduced hazardous waste by 60 percent and saved more than $10 million in disposal costs. And the company plans to spend $500 million in the next five to seven years for further air-quality improvements.

The SMART program prevents pollution by

- Reducing waste generated at the source and recycling what cannot be eliminated.
- Replacing toxic materials and processes with non-toxic alternatives.
- Devising safer operating procedures to reduce the number of petroleum spills, chemical releases, and other accidents.
- Seeking more efficient ways of using materials, and preventing transfer of pollution from one form to another.
- Installing a $22-million stormwater collection and treatment system.

Chevron refinery established a process for recovering hydrocarbons from hazardous wastes. The process uses heat from the refinery's co-generation plant to vaporize hydrocarbons so they can be returned to the crude oil stream.

Dow Chemical's "Waste Reduction Always Pays" (WRAP) program aims to reduce wastes, increase production efficiencies and save costs at all production facilities. It is also a way of recognizing the environmental efforts of employees. WRAP teams drawn from many areas of the company administer this program.

A typical project in the program is at the Glycol plant in Plaquemine, Louisiana. The WRAP team designed a new, closed-loop absorber-water cooling system using high-efficiency heat exchangers and a recycling storage tank to replace a conventional water-cooling tower open to the atmosphere. The process uses less water and eliminates a significant loss of ethylene glycol to the atmosphere.

Since 1974 Dow has reduced total air emissions by 85 percent and increased production by 42 percent. By 1995, it hopes to cut emissions to 50 percent of the 1990 level. By establishing advanced water-treatment systems, it has cut organic discharges into the water by 95 percent in the past 15 years.

These examples of successful waste management are impressive, but not uncommon in industry today. Many companies have developed equally effective programs, even in traditionally dirty industries. That companies are moving toward ecologically beneficial practices is an encouraging sign. However, greening is not uniform. A few companies exhibit environmental leadership, and many simply comply with regulations. Still more companies are struggling to figure out the complex maze of regulations and cope with public pressures for greening.

KEY THEORY E PROPOSITIONS

1. Successful greening requires a *life-cycle approach* that simultaneously changes the company's vision, inputs, throughputs, and outputs.

2. The main focus for greening inputs is to *conserving energy and material resources*. This can be accomplished with simple conservation technologies and substitution of raw materials.

3. Greening the throughput system involves *improving energy and materials productivity* by creating supportive organizational systems and structures. It also requires implementing comprehensive SHE policies and preventing pollution.

4. Environmental programs can save costs and add to revenues. There are many sources of *ecological efficiencies* in corporations.

5. Greening outputs calls for designing products with reduced life-cycle impact on the environment. It also requires *reducing, reusing, and recycling wastes.*

Green Tools
and Processes

Companies have adopted many innovative processes to achieve greening. For greening to be long-lasting and deep, however, companies must address certain internal and external processes and structures. This chapter describes tools that can aid in greening companies.

Internally, environmental concerns must permeate all aspects of work in an organization. This calls for, first, revising the basic values and culture of the organization to accept environmentalism as an important driving force. Second is integrating environmental issues into planning processes: Environmental problems must be addressed in both long-term strategic planning and short-term budgeting. Third, technological innovation must be managed to incorporate ecological conservation.

Externally, organizations must open two-way communication with stakeholders to understand their needs and perceptions and to discuss corporate programs with them. Then, since environmental issues invariably involve conflicts and controversies, companies must create processes for conflict resolution. Finally, companies can cooperate with one another by creating networks to address industry-wide ecological matters. These cooperative relationships can simplify environmental solutions and reduce the environmental damage done by all the member companies.

INTEGRATED GREENING

Successful greening depends on integrating the management of diverse environmental issues into a single comprehensive program. Environmental problems are intertwined with other organizational issues. Resolving these problems in isolation simply fragments them. Fragmented solutions cannot lead to effective greening because they shift environmental effects from one organizational area to another. For example, an environmentally friendly product design may require a manufacturing technology that produces more hazardous wastes.

Fragmented efforts are not perceived as genuine or serious. A company that sells green products at the same time it pollutes the environment is not likely to be believed by stakeholders. Thus, environmental responses must permeate all corporate activities. This gives the company a uniformly green image.

In greening, managers face many trade-offs between costs and benefits, future returns and current savings, growth and consolidation, short term versus long term results, different types of risks and pollution, and competing demands of stakeholders or internal divisions.

Successful greening requires balancing the positive and negative effects of corporate environmental efforts—resolving conflicts and controversies and doing enough to make a significant difference without going overboard. Maintaining a steady, balanced pace prevents disruption in a period of fundamental change.

Many companies do environmental audits and depend on scientific and rational analyses to decide on these trade-offs. Procter & Gamble spent several hundred million dollars in scientific research to address the "phosphate in detergents" issue. The company relied on scientific analysis to answer questions about harm caused by phosphate. It used R&D to develop phosphate-free products. It used scientific consumer research to develop its marketing strategies. These were all effective tool in deciding controversial trade-offs.

Environmental audits can be a useful tool for identifying ecological concerns associated with company operations. The flowcharts in Figure 13.1 show the activities involved in assessing environmental impact. Such assessment typically goes this way:

1. Take stock of existing environmental conditions.
2. Understand how the environment would change or evolve by itself.
3. Assess the environmental impact of several alternative projects and activities.
4. Evaluate and communicate these environmental impacts. Here it is important to share findings on environmental impacts with affected communities and with relevant government agencies. As the result of such discussion, projects should be modified to minimize environmental concerns.
5. Develop plans for preventing environmental damage.
6. Implement and monitor these plans to ensure desirable environmental performance.

The right-side flowchart in Figure 13.1 shows the tasks managers must perform in an environmental audit.

THE USES OF SCIENTIFIC ANALYSIS

Today, the use of scientific analysis alone is not sufficient. There are many differing scientific explanations for controversial environmental problems, and the public often gets confused about which science to believe. In dealing with controversies, corporate scientists are frequently pitted against government scientists, or scientists representing the interest of environmentalists or other independent investigators. In short, science is no longer a compelling and credible arbiter of environmental controversies. Corporations need alternative bases for making trade-offs. One approach is engaging stakeholders in an open discussion to reach mutually acceptable solutions.

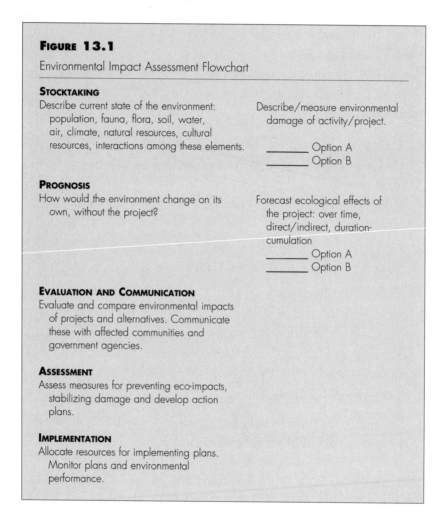

FIGURE 13.1

Environmental Impact Assessment Flowchart

STOCKTAKING

Describe current state of the environment: population, fauna, flora, soil, water, air, climate, natural resources, cultural resources, interactions among these elements.

Describe/measure environmental damage of activity/project.

_____ Option A
_____ Option B

PROGNOSIS

How would the environment change on its own, without the project?

Forecast ecological effects of the project: over time, direct/indirect, duration-cumulation

_____ Option A
_____ Option B

EVALUATION AND COMMUNICATION

Evaluate and compare environmental impacts of projects and alternatives. Communicate these with affected communities and government agencies.

ASSESSMENT

Assess measures for preventing eco-impacts, stabilizing damage and develop action plans.

IMPLEMENTATION

Allocate resources for implementing plans. Monitor plans and environmental performance.

An important aspect of maintaining balance in greening efforts is to keep the process voluntary. Genuine greening cannot be coerced. It cannot be imposed from the top or from the outside. It must emerge from within the company. However, the roles of the CEO and top management in legitimating and encouraging environmental programs should not be underestimated. Without their explicit support, genuine and sustained efforts are unlikely.

There is a minimum threshold of greening activities, below which environmental reforms simply do not take hold. This threshold occurs when employees become convinced of the seriousness of environmental programs. Employees must believe that corporate environmentalism is not simply a fad, or a response to public pressures. They must be convinced of the company's long-term commitment to environmental protection—that the company is willing to reform its values and culture in order to be genuinely green.

GREENING ORGANIZATIONAL CULTURE AND STRUCTURE

Greening of corporations must first involve change in their basic values. The corporate culture must become ecocentric. It must come to value nature, natural resources, and natural processes.

Some of the fundamental values about the relationship of humans to nature that underlie our culture and corporations are in direct conflict with ecocentrism. Our culture values individualism, unrestrained consumerism, anthropocentrism. These values conflict with the view of humans as part of nature, in harmonious coexistence with it. Table 13.1 shows some of the differences between traditional and ecocentric values.

Corporate cultural changes should be made in order to sensitize managers to ecocentric values. These values form a different way of looking at the world. Such a perspective locates firms, markets, and economies in an evolutionary biological-geological-ecological system.

An ecological perspective requires knowing and understanding the Earth's ecology. It can also emerge from personal experience; for example, such commonplace experiences of nature as hiking, gardening, and sailing, can evoke strong positive feelings about nature. Thus, combining ecological knowledge and personal experience is a useful first step in realizing and accepting ecological values.

To develop corporate cultures that are sensitive to ecology, companies must go beyond the personal acceptance of such

TABLE 13.1

Traditional versus Ecocentric Values

VALUES ABOUT	TRADITIONAL	ECOCENTRIC
Humans	Individualism	Part of a community
	Self-interest	Community interest
	Independence	Interdependence
	Hierarchical relationships	Web-like relationships
Nature	Inanimate	Living system
	External, separate from humans	Part of the human community
	Exploitable	Symbiotic
Relationship of humans to nature	Anthropocentrism	Harmonious co-existence
	Subdue and conquer nature	Renew and conserve nature

values by managers to institutionalizing the values in policies, procedures, and structures. Corporate ecological values must be stated in an environmental mission statement and environmental policies. The CEO and other top managers should show support for these missions and policies.

In addition, some companies have found "environmental involvement" exercises useful for developing ecological values. General Electric and other companies use Outward Bound programs to develop environmental appreciation, interpersonal skills, team spirit, and camaraderie among managers. Other companies encourage environmental activism as a way of reinforcing environmental values. Employees at The Body Shop, Procter & Gamble, and Ben & Jerry's take part in environmental and social projects in their communities. The Body Shop makes such personal environmental projects a part of employees' formal job contract.

Rewarding environmental performance is a powerful way of signaling institutional approval. Green companies use rewards and peer recognition to encourage employees. The celebration of ecological accomplishments is a great motivating force. Many companies, including 3M and Ben & Jerry's, provide monetary rewards and public acknowledgment to workers who make outstanding environmental contributions. These rewards strongly reinforce ecological values and commitments.

Finally, ecologically sensitive values and cultures must be supported with compatible organizational structures. These structures should promote environmentally responsive decisions at all levels. Such structures seek to empower employees and encourage grass-roots employee initiatives. In keeping with ecocentric values, they de-emphasize hierarchy and emphasize inclusion, equality, and participation.

Ecocentric organizational structures are not easily introduced in traditional, hierarchical organizations. Such companies can resort to "matrix" structures, in which environmental responsibilities overlap line managers and environmental staff. Procter & Gamble operates with a successful matrix structure. Operating plant personnel are responsible for environmental programs. They receive advice and research support from a centralized staff of environmental specialists. An environmental department at corporate headquarters provides research and communication support to product design and marketing departments and to operating units.

Formal structures can be augmented with temporary and informal task forces, committees, or project teams. Such temporary structures are particularly useful for initiating environmental programs. They allow a special group to work within existing structures. Once their efforts start paying off, it is easier to create formal or permanent structures.

Companies have also found special "eco-events"—a group retreat or a company picnic—useful for launching environmental programs. Some companies use media events and other high-visibility public occasions to announce major environmental initiatives. Such events galvanize the attention of employees and external stakeholders. They also help to institutionalize ecological commitments by making them public.

Accepting ecological improvement as a corporate value requires corresponding changes in all aspects of the company. Cultural change in the direction of ecological sensitivity is a continuous and an ongoing process.

GREENING ORGANIZATIONAL PLANNING

The second organizational process that supports greening is organizational planning. Companies that are successful in greening use planning processes that energize employee participation. Workers are the best source of ideas for improving ecological performance. They know their jobs, the possibilities for change, and the barriers to change. Planning is a good vehicle for encouraging workers to articulate, review, and implement ideas for ecological improvement.

Organizational planning for greening includes long-range strategic planning, product planning, and annual budget planning.

Strategic Planning

At this level of planning, a company must ensure that it is creating a future for itself that is compatible with ecological limits and problems. Companies can use portfolio analysis to identify unusual sources of environmental risks. For example, such analysis could have identified the unusually high risk posed by the Bhopal plant of the Union Carbide Corporation. Planners can use the analytical techniques of risk management, environmental impact assessment, crisis/emergency management, and early warning systems to identify likely sources of risk, and contingency planning to help mitigate risks and prepare for emergencies.

Planning for ecological concerns should be integrated into the formal strategic planning system. This can be done using the following broad steps:

1. Establish environmental missions and objectives.
2. Analyze the ecological problems facing the industry and specific business units.
3. Assess corporate strengths, resources, and weaknesses. What financial, human, and technological strengths can the company use for solving ecological problems?

4. Integrate ecological issues in the choice of corporate and competitive business strategies. Develop a corporate ecology strategy. Develop corporate SHE policies.
5. Implement ecology-related policies and programs. Allocate necessary resources and staff, develop systems and structures, create skills, and provide strategic leadership to make ecological programs happen.
6. Evaluate, monitor, and modify environmental programs periodically. Ensure that they are meeting the objectives originally set.

Product Planning

Product planning can serve as a useful tool for greening. The choice of products sharply influences the ecological impacts of the company. It determines raw materials and energy needs, and the nature of production technologies. Product impact audit and product life-cycle assessment help in understanding these influences.

Budget Planning

In the short run the annual budgeting process can be an ally of greening. The budget planning cycle is the logical vehicle for allocating financial resources for ecological projects, from both operating and capital budgets. Budgeting also provides an occasion to question cost of operations, and seek more cost-effective and ecologically sound ways of doing business.

: In some companies there is a close link between the budget process and accounts auditing. The auditing system can be expanded to include environmental audits. Just as accounts auditors verify the soundness of accounts, environmental auditors assess and verify the corporation's environmental liabilities (and assets). Such audits can identify potential ecological problems, and enable the company to take preemptive remedial action. Many environmental auditing guides are available for general corporate and industry-specific uses.

PRODUCT LIFE-CYCLE ASSESSMENT CHECKLIST

The purpose of this assessment is to understand the cradle-to-grave costs and environmental impacts of products. The following steps can help you in conducting such an assessment.

☑ Define the steps involved in producing, consuming or using, and disposing of the product, in terms of concept design, R&D, raw material extraction and processing, production processes, transportation, use and consumption, and post-use disposal treatments.

☑ For each step, identify the materials used, materials wasted, and total materials consumed. Similarly, identify energy used and total energy consumed in processing, and transportation energy.

☑ Set up a spreadsheet and sum the materials/energy used. Convert to a common cost unit to get the total product life-cycle cost.

☑ For each step, identify the environmental impact in terms of materials consumed, pollution, waste, risks produced, and long-term ecological effects.

☑ Identify ecological opportunities for saving materials and energy, using substitute materials, reducing environmental impact, and minimizing overall costs.

Procter & Gamble has established a unique Total-Environmental Quality-Management system. It covers the environmental implications of a product over its entire life cycle. It ties environmental quality together with diverse internal processes (budgeting, strategic planning, operational planning, procurement planning, research and development, etc.). It subtly incorporates environmental considerations into product design, product planning, production, packaging, distribution, promotion and merchandising, and product disposal.

3M is another example of a company that puts environmental responsiveness into all aspects of its operations. 3M has combined resources from diverse departments to create "conservation technologies" in energy and resource conservation, waste management, and pollution control.

INNOVATION IN CONSERVATION TECHNOLOGIES

Gearing technological processes to conservation can be a powerful tool for greening. Technological processes include systems and programs that generate new products and production methods. They encompass operating and administrative procedures in R&D, engineering, product development and management, manufacturing, and training.

Conservation technologies and innovations must pass critical appraisal not only on market and financial criteria, but also on environmental, safety, and health criteria. It is not essential for conservation innovations to be high-tech and expensive. They can be low-tech and commonsense changes. Examples from the electronics and energy industries illustrate this.

The electronics industry was a major user of ozone-destroying CFCs. Nearly 33 percent of CFC production was used for cleaning printed circuit boards. AT&T, Apple Computer, and Northern Telecom devised a cleaning mixture made from orange peels and detergents to substitute for CFCs. They changed the production process in ways that minimize the need for cleaning. The new cleaning systems are technologically simpler, environmentally cleaner, less expensive, and safer than those using CFCs. This innovation will soon enable the industry to eliminate the use of CFCs entirely.

The energy industry boasts even simpler technologies used for energy conservation—fluorescent bulbs, automatic light switches, regular maintenance, passive solar building construction, and shifting use of electricity to off-peak hours.

Technological innovations can solve many environmental problems, but they often create others. A good example of this is pesticides, which are a great boon to agriculture. They kill pests that destroy nearly 30 percent of food in some countries. However, overuse, misuse, and abuse of pesticides is responsible for thousands of pesticide-poisoning deaths and injuries each year. Pesticides contaminate human food, injure wildlife, and over the long term lose their effectiveness as pests mutate to resistant forms.

Environmentalists have developed a healthy skepticism toward technological solutions. In this era where technology itself is suspect, corporations need conservation-oriented innovations. They can encourage this by using conservation as a criterion for selecting new projects.

The shifting focus of internal organizational processes toward environmental protection must be accompanied by changes in external processes. Here, communication with external stakeholders, conflict management, and cooperation with other companies are vital.

STAKEHOLDER COMMUNICATION

Stakeholder communication is a fundamental part of corporate greening. Communication programs should provide information about corporate greening to all relevant stakeholders. External stakeholders need to know about corporate environmental efforts, and companies need to know about environmental demands by its external stakeholders, who include communities near company facilities, environmental public-interest groups, government agencies, customers, shareholders, employees, the public, and the media.

These groups need many different types of information. Government agencies need information mandated by law. Customers may want information on the health and environmental effects of products and the presence of hazardous ingredients. Shareholders want to know about financial liability for environmental and product-harm incidents. Communities and environmental activists may want quantitative data on discharge and emissions and their effect on public and environmental safety. They may want to know about emergency plans in case of accidents.

Stakeholder communications programs should be able to meet these diverse needs. Compliance programs distribute hazard information required by law. Other programs deal with community risk communication, consumer education, emergency planning and coordination, and media/public relations.

Prototypes for most of these programs are now widely available through industry associations. In the chemical industry, the U.S.-based Chemical Manufacturers Association has established the "Responsible Care" program. CEFIC, the European Chemical Industry Federation, has its "Guidelines for the Communication of Environmental Information." And the United Nations has expanded these programs internationally through its APPEL program. (See the checklist on environmental communications.)

One important role of stakeholder communication is to elicit ideas for making products more desirable to customers. Many companies have received their best environmental ideas from open communication with customers, suppliers, and regulators. Procter & Gamble developed its dehydrated version of Tide in response to consumer preference for ecologically sound packaging. Johnson & Johnson uses inputs from customers and retailers to create safe and eco-friendly products and packaging.

An unfortunate early trend in greening has been toward propaganda. Some corporations have taken a cynical view of greening and used it as a public relations tool. Glossy brochures and television ads heralding environmental achievements are now commonplace. Many companies claim unverifiable environmental benefits for their products and programs. Examples include the biodegradable garbage bag and disposable diapers that are supposed to degrade in landfills but do not, due to lack of sunlight. The public has grown wary of such rhetoric.

AN ENVIRONMENTAL COMMUNICATION CHECKLIST

- ☑ Communicate environmental missions and programs to employees in all parts of the company. A videotaped message from the CEO on the company's environmental philosophy is an effective tool for raising employee awareness.

- ☑ Establish a two-way communications program with communities in which the company operates. Provide opportunities for community members to express their environmental concerns.

- ☑ Communicate environmental emergency procedures and plans to relevant community agencies (hospitals, police, state department of environment, etc.).

- ☑ Communicate environmental missions, programs, and achievements to the media for public dissemination.

- ☑ Use a combination of communication vehicles to achieve your objectives. These may include memos, internal documents, press releases and kits, brochures, videos, advertising, and direct marketing.

- ☑ Publish an annual environmental report that describes the company's environmental practices and accomplishments.

- ☑ Communicate environmental efforts to other corporate stakeholders, including investors, financial analysts, bankers, customers, suppliers, and business associates.

- ☑ Establish a comprehensive regulatory communication program to cover mandatory environmental, safety and health reporting, emissions notification, site permits, and other legal requirements.

Many non-governmental and government programs are now available to standardize environmental performance claims of products. These include, Greenseal in the United States, Blue Angel in Germany, and Eco Mark in Japan, which is issued by the Japan Environmental Association. Several Japanese cities, including Tokyo, Kawasaki, Yokohama, and Fujizawa, have initiated "Eco-shops," a program certifying retail stores that follow high ecological standards.

Even the most comprehensive communication program is unlikely to eliminate all conflicts and controversies inherent in environmental issues. The science behind solving ecological problems is not perfect. In addition, the ecological values of corporate stakeholders vary widely. Consequently, despite many years of research and political debate, there is little consensus on ecological solutions. Considering this reality, it is necessary for corporate greening to address ecological conflicts.

Conflict Management

Unfortunately, conflicts are a recurring feature of organizational attempts to be ecologically responsive. External stakeholders may disagree about the extent, direction, and priorities for greening adopted by a company. Vocal and aggressive environmental groups engage companies in debates and lawsuits over ecological problems. Consumers are suing companies for product injuries. Government agencies must follow ever more stringent standards and impose high fines on errant companies. Internal conflicts occur among divisions, departments, and individuals who place different priorities and values on greening efforts. And greening actions worsen the traditional conflict between profitable growth and expenditures (in this case, for green programs).

In short, greening is a conflict-ridden activity. Companies must learn to handle these conflicts constructively. They cannot afford to become too defensive. They cannot simply use financial and political muscle to suppress conflict or resort to expensive and time-consuming litigation. Instead, corporations need to develop a thoughtful approach to conflict management, so that they can distinguish between different types of conflicts and engage each in appropriate ways. Some conflicts can be resolved by issue management and communication with stakeholders. Others may be settled through third-party mediation. Still others may need to go to litigation.

- Strategic-issues management can help companies to track and shape ecological issues that have potential for generating conflict. This requires studying and monitoring ecological issues from their early stages, before they become problems. Companies can thus engage and shape the debate on the issue as it develops.
- Many third-party mediation alternatives for environmental dispute resolution have emerged in the past decade. Examples include arbitration, environmental mediation, joint conciliation, and use of neutral independent observers or commissions.
- Litigation remains the last resort. In environmental conflicts, litigation is usually very costly, time-consuming, and unsatisfactory for all parties. The conflicts are usually complex, requiring protracted and expensive legal battles.

Companies also need to establish procedures for resolving internal conflicts. Most companies already have some form of internal conflict-resolution system which can be used for environmental conflicts as well. However, it may be beneficial to establish in addition an environmental ombudsman. The ombudsman could be a committee or managerial group with ecological, business, and technical expertise. Its task would be to mediate environmental conflicts by making acceptable trade-offs.

Just as there is potential for conflicts, ecological issues also offer potential for cooperation. The next section examines the possibilities for ecological cooperation among companies.

INDUSTRIAL ECOLOGY NETWORKS

Some ecological solutions require cooperation of various kinds among companies. Sharing information is one, usually carried on through industry associations. This is particularly true in such environment-sensitive industries as chemicals, oil, paper, and forest products. The Chemical Manufacturers Association and American Petroleum Institute, for example, keep their members up to date on environmental developments in their industries.

Beyond information sharing, there is the sharing of technologies and managerial practices. The electronics industry widely shares technology for replacing CFCs as a cleaning agent. The Global Environmental Management Initiative (GEMI) shares the best practices of firms that are ecological leaders with other companies.

The idea of "industrial ecology networks" or "industrial ecosystems" has emerged in recent years to describe a unique form of ecological cooperation. The industrial ecosystem idea parallels the natural ecosystem, in which interdependent organisms and their environments exchange resources with each other to survive.

For example, in a marine ecosystem, big fish eat little fish, little fish eat insects, insects eat weeds and plankton. The waste products of the fishes serve as resources for the growth of weeds, plankton, and fish habitats. This arrangement forms a self-sufficient, dynamically balanced ecosystem.

As a parallel, the industrial ecosystem consists of a network of organizations that jointly seek to minimize environmental degradation. They use each other's waste, and share and minimize the use of natural resources.

A network of companies in Kalundborg, Denmark, demonstrates what an industrial ecosystem is. It consists of a power plant, an enzyme plant, a refinery, a chemical plant, and a wallboard plant. These plants use one another's wastes and by-products as raw materials. They coordinate their use of resources and waste-management practices. Figure 13.2 shows the flow of resources between them.

The coal-fired Asnaes power plant sells its used steam to the Novo Nordisk enzyme plant and the Statoil refinery, instead of condensing it and dumping it into the sea. The power plant also

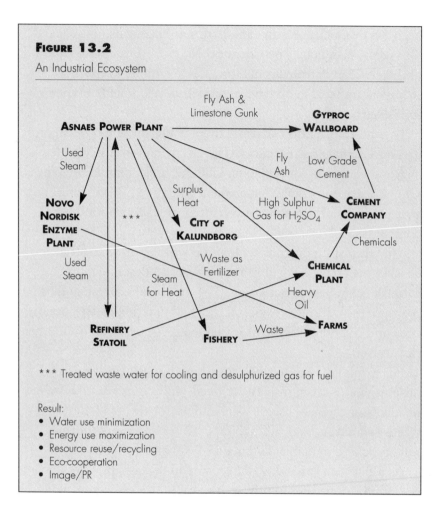

FIGURE 13.2

An Industrial Ecosystem

*** Treated waste water for cooling and desulphurized gas for fuel

Result:
- Water use minimization
- Energy use maximization
- Resource reuse/recycling
- Eco-cooperation
- Image/PR

sells its fly ash to a cement company, and surplus heat to the city for heating. Statoil in turn supplies Asnaes with treated wastewater for cooling. It also sells the power plant desulphurized gas to burn, saving 30,000 tons of coal a year. The plant then ships high-sulphur gas emissions to a sulphuric acid plant. Asnaes removes pollutants from its smokestacks and sells the limestone gunk to Gyproc, the wallboard plant. This cuts the imports of mined gypsum. Asnaes warms a fishery that produces 200 tons of trout and turbot each year. Local farms use waste from the fishery and from Novo's enzyme plant as fertilizer.

The impact of this industrial ecosystem on the natural environment is impressive. It conserves water that is pumped from Lake Tisso, seven miles away. It minimizes the amount of waste sent to landfills. It reduces the pollution that would otherwise be emitted into the atmosphere. It conserves energy resources in the community. It gets companies to cooperate on ecological problems and provides a forum for ongoing improved environmental performance. In addition, it provides participant companies with good image-making publicity.

Viewing organizations as a part of an industrial ecosystem necessitates many fundamental changes in a company's concept of itself. It requires a new vision of operational scope, strategies, cost structures, location, and management practices. It requires very different criteria for new product development, venture financing, entrepreneurial forms, and infrastructure. It requires rethinking the role of regulations and markets, and creating fresh markets for ecologically sound products.

SUMMARY

The internal and external organizational processes discussed in this chapter can provide the vehicle for corporate greening. In summary, here are their salient features:

1. Greening must be integrated into (must permeate) all business areas and levels in a balanced way, so that it does not disrupt operations. For this to occur, companies need to change both internal and external processes.
2. Change in the values and culture of a company is a requirement for corporate greening.
3. Strategic planning, product planning, and budgeting systems must explicitly address environmental issues. There must be guidelines for making risk/benefit trade-offs.

4. Technological and administrative innovation for ecological conservation are a potent tool for greening.
5. Environmental programs should be shared with external audiences through an open, two-way stakeholder communications program.
6. Conflicts and controversies over environment, safety, and health issues are endemic and cannot be avoided. Companies will benefit by establishing conflict-management processes to deal with these strategic issues.
7. Ecosystem networks of companies in an industry allow groups of companies to reduce their total impact on the ecology. Companies can cooperatively solve ecological problems that may not be solvable otherwise.

Toward Second-Order Greening

T he themes addressed in previous chapters are essentially reformist. They take existing corporations as a point of departure and seek to modify their corporate behavior incrementally. However, such reformism can be attacked as not addressing the nature-exploiting character of modern corporations—and industrialism in general. The reforms could be interpreted as being useful but not deep enough to make a real difference. They could even be viewed as placatory, cosmetic, and hence maintaining the status quo.

One answer to such criticism lies in providing a vision for radically green corporations of the future—a vision based on fundamentally different assumptions about growth, resource use, environmental protection, and ownership. This chapter describes the key characteristics of such companies, calling them *bioregionally sustainable multinational corporations*. (*Bioregion* refers to a geographical area that is part of a coherent ecosystem.)

Admittedly, at this time this is only a vision. For the vision to become reality, changes must be made not only in corporations, but also in individuals and in society. Individuals need to reevaluate their personal relationships with nature and its consequences for their lifestyles. As a society, we need collective action (regulations, institutions, norms) that will support ecological sustainability.

At first glance, "bioregionally sustainable multinational corporations" (BioCorp for short) may seem a contradiction. But it *is* possible to create multinational companies in this mold. A BioCorp consists of many small, autonomous units, voluntarily allocates resources to environmental enhancement, and uses bioregional resources in an environmentally sustainable manner. It is a company that has a non-alienating work environment, and makes community welfare its central concern. In the future this may be the only feasible ecologically sustainable corporate form. The challenge facing captains of industry and policy-makers of the coming decade is to make such corporations a reality.

THE CHANGING WORLD CONTEXT

The vision of a BioCorp makes sense only in a specific world context. The context consists of several related strategic changes:

1. The globalization of corporations.
2. Expansion of ecological risks and degradation from industrial activities.
3. Local social resistance to activity that creates environmental problems.

This context, still emerging, will have a high degree of interdependence among global and local concerns. In the world of the future, global problems will require local solutions, and vice versa. The world economic order has been moving inexorably toward an integrated, interdependent global economy. The use of computer and telecommunications technology has integrated world financial markets. Today money transfers and financial transactions can be conducted almost instantaneously. The top 100 international banks, along with the World Bank, control more than 70 percent of the international money flow.

Labor has been experiencing similar trends toward globalization for the past two decades. Millions of workers have moved from their home countries to new job locations. In some countries there are more foreign workers than indigenous ones. More than 5 million workers from the Middle East now work in Europe. More than 7 million workers from developing countries such as India, Pakistan, and Bangladesh, and from poor Arab countries, work in oil-rich states such as Kuwait and Saudi Arabia. Millions of workers from Mexico and other Central American countries have moved to the United States.

Another factor in global economic integration is the conversion of the former European Eastern Bloc countries to market economies. These new "free" markets are linking up with Western market economies. This is bringing the majority of world population into a single, interconnected global economic system.

In addition, regional market alliances are integrating the economies of groups of countries. In 1992, the European Common Market integrated the economies of 12 countries and it continues to expand. The North American Free Trade Agreement (NAFTA) between Canada, the United States, and Mexico has created another unified market. Japan and its Pacific neighbors are banding together in a regional economic alliance. Brazil, Argentina, Paraguay, and Uruguay have formed Mercudor, their own regional market. The oil-producing countries coordinate their economic policies through the Organization of Petroleum Exporting Countries (OPEC).

Nearly all major companies today are multinational. Many large ones, such as Compaq Computers, Honda Motors, IBM, Shell Oil, and Volvo Car Company make more than half their revenues and profits outside their home countries. In 1993, the world GNP was about $3 trillion, nearly 70 percent of it produced by the top 1,000 multinational corporations. These companies have global production and distribution, global finance, and global administration.

The second defining feature of the future corporate context is expansion of environmental degradation. Chapter 1 argued that in post-industrial societies ecological risks occur simultaneously with the production of wealth. The ecological degradation produced per unit of wealth is increasing, and now often exceeds the wealth produced. This degradation is expanding at an exponential rate as the world economy grows.

Environmental problems are becoming at once globally extensive in scope and locally intensive in effect. Global environmental problems such as ozone depletion, global warming, deforestation, desertification, and declining biodiversity are now well recognized. Even problems that were largely domestic are becoming international. For example, toxic waste disposal is spilling over into the export of hazardous wastes. Industrial accidents such as Chernobyl and Bhopal have very serious effects across natural and national boundaries. Air pollution and acid rain are now clearly international problems.

Even as these problems become global in scope, they also intensify in local effect. Cleanup costs are rising—the revised Clean Air Act of 1991 requires American companies to spend an additional $30 to $50 billion on environmental protection measures. The health effects of environmental pollution are becoming more apparent, and real estate prices have become sensitized to environmental concerns.

This expanding and intensifying environmental degradation demands BioCorps in all regions of the world. That means the economic activities of any region must be guided by bioregional demand and supply, and more importantly, by their natural resource and sink capacities. Exceeding the bioregional capacities of natural resources and sinks has been a source of ecological imbalance and degradation in the past.

The final element of the context for future corporations is the role of *social movements and struggles for environmental preservation and eco-justice*. The environmental movement is likely to be a main and growing source of resistance to the economic exploitation of natural resources. Environmentalism is no longer on the fringes of society. In North America and Western Europe, it has quietly become a solidly middle-class movement focused on preserving the quality of life. In developing countries, it is a political movement for the survival of people dependent on common natural resources. In the former Soviet Union, it is gaining ground rapidly as a protection against rapacious ecological exploitation.

In addition, a broad range of sympathetic social movements are becoming environmentally conscious. These include urbanism, feminism, consumerism, the civil rights movement, and the labor movement. The state of the natural environment affects all of these groups—urbanites, women, consumers, minorities, and workers. It is true that each movement has its own agenda. However, they are also taking positions on environmental degradation, industrial safety, and public health.

Collectively, these movements are formidable forces reshaping the environmental behaviors of individuals and organizations. They demand basic changes in the management and structure of corporations, including reorientation of ownership, changing forms of production, eco-friendly products tailored to local needs, and socially acceptable work conditions. These demands involve moving corporations beyond *market* and *profit* to a concern for *environment* and *community*.

THE BIOCORP

What would an ideal BioCorp be? What kind of products would it produce? Who will own it, and how will it be governed? What types of production and distribution systems would it have? What organizational forms would it adopt? What would be its relationships with stakeholders, communities, and nature?

I envision a BioCorp to be an ecologically stable entity, using natural resources but also providing for renewal of these resources, in order to maintain the ecological balance within its bioregion. It would be an integral part of its bioregional ecology and economy. Such corporations would have a net beneficial impact on preserving eco-resources and socioeconomic security. It would contribute to socially equitable improvements in the quality of life. It would prevent environmental pollution and damage, restore damaged environments to healthy conditions, and seek to operate with high degrees of ecological efficiency.

A BioCorp will have a sustainable organizational form, a community-oriented ownership structure, and relate to other organizations with the ecological logic implicit in industrial ecosystems.

A Sustainable Organizational Form

Key elements of corporations can be characterized by seven S's popularized by Robert Waterman and Tom Peters: strategies, structures, systems, skills, staff, style of management, and superordinate goals (mission and values). These seven S's would take on a special configuration in a BioCorp, which would have internal organizational designs allowing it to be environmentally responsive.

Strategies. Environmentally sensitive corporate and competitive strategies guide a BioCorp to leave environmentally hazardous businesses and enter into eco-friendly ones. This reduces technological risks and environmental hazards associated with operations. At the business-unit level, sustainable strategies produce cost savings through ecological efficiency gains. They differentiate the firm's products from those of its competitors. They have powerful effects on the reputation and goodwill of a firm.

Structures. Appropriate organizational structures and reporting relationships are key elements of the sustainable BioCorp. Instead of traditional hierarchies, it has a flat structure. It encourages decentralized, participative decision-making. Responsibility for such environmentally sensitive functions as environmental protection, worker safety, public safety and health, and technological risk are distributed throughout the organization. In addition, there is an independent and strong environmental affairs department with a direct link to top management. A BioCorp has credible and visible champions for environmental issues within the firm. The board of directors oversees environmental performance.

Systems. A BioCorp will have administrative systems that actively seek out environmental information and are responsive to environmental demands. The design of resource allocation systems, planning and budgeting systems, and management information and control systems is based on environmental criteria. In particular, the life-cycle approach to project analysis and capital budgeting is standard operating procedure. These corporations recognize and reward environmental performance.

Information systems within a BioCorp foster the free flow of information about ecological problems and opportunities. Experience in many industries shows that simply gathering and disseminating environmental information promotes the transfer of learning and spreads best practices across the organization; it also facilitates continuous improvement in environmental performance.

Skills. A successful BioCorp needs skills and technological capabilities, or "core competencies," configured to support its strategy. This requires an internal audit of human skills and capabilities, and the reallocation of resources to those technologies which meet the criteria of "total environmental management." This reallocation includes minimization of energy, material, waste, and life-cycle costs.

Of critical concern to a BioCorp is the quality of its personnel or staff. These organizations pay special attention to hiring and training personnel who have both technical competence and a sincere regard for the natural environment. Training emphasizes environmental values and provides employees with information that allows them to integrate environmental issues into their daily work.

The working environment of a BioCorp is perhaps the major difference between it and the kind of firm that exists today.

Workers are treated not simply as labor or an economic resource for production. They are regarded as complete humans needing, in addition to wages, opportunities for self-actualization and social, cultural, and spiritual fulfillment. Work is not fragmented, demeaning, and alienating. It utilizes the whole individual and is meaningful. It allows employees to meld personal, family, organizational, and professional obligations into a balanced life. Work provides opportunities for creative expression and enhanced self-esteem.

Style. A BioCorp has a style of operation that emphasizes environmental values, a style best reflected in the corporate culture. It encourages what Ian Mitroff and Terry Pauchant label a "crisis-avoiding" culture, that is sensitive to environmental protection and conservation issues. In contrast, "crisis-prone" organizational cultures disregard the natural environment, encourage rigid structures, are overconfident about their technological prowess, and are overly defensive about organizational resources. The cultural values of a BioCorp emphasize harmonious co-existence with the natural world, view humans as part of that natural world, and acknowledge the rights of nature to exist for its own sake.

Superordinate Goals. The goals of a BioCorp include a mission and vision that signals strong environmental norms and values and provides well-articulated principles of behavior. The corporate environmental mission provides the glue which holds together the other elements of organizational design: Alignment of the organization's strategies, structure, systems, and processes is greatly enhanced by a few widely shared values and norms.

Ownership and Control

The trend toward global markets and production will require a successful BioCorp to be international in scope. But unlike the corporations of today, these companies will also have international ownership. Capital will come from multitudes of common-stock owners and investors worldwide.

The relationship of ownership and control will also be different. Modern corporations belong to widely dispersed owners who, for lack of time, inclination, ability, or information, do not involve themselves in management. As a consequence, management exercises control over corporate assets and strategies. Management also strongly influences appointments to boards of directors. Despite recent activism by several boards, most let management have control of the company. This is *managerial capitalism*, in which managers and not owners exercise control.

One consequence of managerial capitalism is lack of sensitivity to local issues. Managers sitting in distant, often foreign, headquarters are far removed from local ecological and social issues. While they may care about these issues, they deal with them only through multiple intermediaries and standard policies. These policies are not tailored to very different local circumstances and needs. Many layers of decision-making separate top management from local issues. Local problems become abstract, and of secondary concern. The main concern remains the financial growth and profitability of the total enterprise. Under these conditions, it is natural to let local interests be sacrificed for global efficiencies.

We are witnessing changes in this model of ownership and control. In 1992, the board of directors of General Motors, one of the world's largest companies, replaced the chief executive officer and shook up the entire management structure. The board was dissatisfied with the pace of change at recession-battered GM. Boards in many American companies are waking up to their fiduciary responsibilities to protect stockholder interests.

Another force for transformation is shareholder activism, on the rise since the mid-1980s. Shareholders are taking back some control over companies in order to achieve social demands. This social activism is one motive for pension funds, labor groups, environmentalists, and consumer groups exerting pressure and winning battles against entrenched managements.

Another relevant trend is the increase in the number of small, medium-size, and new businesses. These entrepreneurial businesses already provide a majority of jobs in the United States and Japan. Entrepreneurship is becoming a preferred career option for women and middle managers. As recession-induced downsizing reduces employment in large corporations, small companies are likely to proliferate.

Small size has the positive effect of making organizations responsive to local needs. The longer-term consequences of these trends will be the emergence of ownership and control patterns that are much more responsive to local, ecological and human concerns. Through the shifting allegiances of socially concerned stockholders, more conscientious boards of directors, and locally concerned smaller companies, bioregional sustainability can become a central objective of companies.

It is often believed that, lacking economies of scale, many small plants in place of a few large ones will be more expensive. This assumption of economies of scale is a myth in many industries and needs to be examined very carefully.

Kirkpatric Sale (1986) has argued that the history of human communities shows that they are capable of economic independence at a population of about 5,000 to 10,000. At this level, agricultural systems, energy systems, and distribution systems can be operated efficiently. This population provides a labor force of 2,000 to 5,000. More importantly, Sale cites the figures shown in the box for how many people it takes (both in the front office and in production) to operate plants in a variety of basic industries. These are amazing numbers, because they support the feasibility of decentralized, community-based, small-scale operations.

Many small plants also provide companies with more flexibility, and the ability to tailor products to local demand. These advantages can more than offset short-term extra costs in particular cases.

WORKERS PER PLANT
(BY INDUSTRY)

Textiles	132
Apparel	56
Lumber and wood products	29
Furniture and fixtures	50
Paper and allied products	104
Soap, cleaners, toiletries	43
Stone clay and glass products	39
Primary metal industry	163
Fabricated metal products	50
Machinery (except electrical)	45
Electrical and electronic equipment	135
Motorcycles, bicycles, parts	81
Instruments and related products	75

To enhance the ability of business to respond to local concerns, even large corporations can be administratively organized into many small units, each unit consisting of a few hundred employees. These units would be profit centers, responsible to local managers and responding to local concerns.

Bioregional Industrial Ecology

A BioCorp will be organized in a manner consistent with the bioregional industrial ecology. Each region is endowed with certain natural resources, demand patterns, and waste disposal options. The term "bio-regional industrial ecology" refers to creating production and distribution systems that are consistent with these local characteristics. The industrial ecology concept, as explained earlier, attempts to model industrial organizations on ecological systems. Within such an ecology, companies relate to each other through ecological interdependencies. Companies use each other's wastes and by-products collectively to reduce resource and energy consumption as well as waste and ecological impact.

A Biocorp operating in an industrial ecology will encourage the use of locally available resources in quantities that are ecologically sustainable, to satisfy local and regional demands. It will use as inputs natural resources and the wastes and by-products of firms in the region. Simultaneously, companies will make provision for renewing the natural resource base of the region. This may involve sustainable cultivation of resources, use of renewable energy resources, and creation of renewable substitute materials.

Production systems will be decentralized, consisting of many small plants specialized to meet local and regional demands. Such reorganization of production will also reduce transportation costs and improve local employment conditions. Waste disposal from production facilities will be tied into a regional waste management system. This system will make judicious use of landfills, incineration, and in-ground and waterway disposal of wastes.

OUTLOOK FOR THE FUTURE

Creating bioregionally sustainable business networks requires long-term planning. Time horizons will extend over several decades rather than the typical three to five years. Such planning should also be bioregionally directed: It should consider economic, social, and political issues within a bioregional framework. And it should incorporate multiple stakeholder needs.

For corporations to achieve the ideal of sustainability, they must be supported by appropriate incentives and pressures from outside. A variety of "instruments of sustainability" can be brought to bear on corporations to speed their conversion. These include government regulations, incentives and fines, environmental taxes, and outside financing for environmental projects and programs.

Governments around the world are just beginning to put these instruments of change into place. The July 1992 United Nations Conference on Environment and Development in Brazil enacted many international environmental treaties. Over time, these will lead to new laws in each country. As these laws begin taking effect, we can look with hope towards an era of ecologically sustainable business enterprise.

Bibliography

Allenby, B. R. *Industrial ecology*. New York: Prentice Hall, 1993.

Ayres, R. U., and U. Simonis, eds. *Industrial metabolism*. Tokyo: United Nations University Press, 1992.

Agarwal, A. *The state of India's environment*. New Delhi: Center for Environment and Development, 1988.

Beck, U. *Risk society: towards a new modernity*. Thousand Oaks, CA: Sage, 1992.

Bell, D. *The coming of post-industrial society*. New York: Basic Books, 1973.

Berry, T. *Dream of the earth*. San Francisco: Sierra Club Books, 1988.

Binswanger, M. "From microscopic to macroscopic theories: Entropic aspects of ecological and economic processes." *Ecological Economics* 8, No. 3 (1993):209–234.

Bowonder, B., J. X. Kasperson, and R. E. Kasperson. "Industrial risk management in India after Bhopal." In S. Jasanoff, ed., *Learning from disaster: Policy consequences of Bhopal*. Philadelphia: University of Pennsylvania Press, 1994.

Brion, D. *Essential industry and the NIMBY phenomenon*. New York: Quorum Books, 1991.

Brown, Lester, and staff of the Worldwatch Institute. *State of the World*. New York: W. W. Norton, 1987, 1988, 1989, 1990, 1991, 1992, 1993.

Brown, L., C. Flavin, and H. Kanes. *Vital signs, 1992: trends that are shaping our future*. New York: W. W. Norton, 1992.

Bucholz, R. A. *Principles of environmental management*. Englewood Cliffs, NJ: Prentice Hall, 1993.

Bucholz, R., A. Marcus, and J. Post. *Managing environmental issues: a case book*. Englewood Cliffs, NJ: Prentice Hall, 1992.

Burrel, G., and G. Morgan. *Sociological paradigms and organizational analysis*. London: Heinemann, 1978.

Buzzelli, D. "Time to structure an environmental policy strategy." *The Journal of Business Strategy* (March/April 1991):17–20.

Cairncross, F. *Costing the earth*. Cambridge: Harvard University Press, 1992.

Callenbach, E., F. Capra, L. Goldman, R. Lutz, and S. Marburg. *Eco-Management*. San Francisco: Barrett Koehler, 1993.

Campbell, A., and S. Yeung. "Creating a sense of mission." *Long Range Planning*, 1991, 24:10–20.

Carroll, J. E. "A three-dimensional conceptual model of corporate social performance." *Academy of Management Review* 4 (1979):497–505.

Carson, P., and J. Moulden. *Green is gold*. New York: Harper-Business, 1991.

Carson, R. *Silent Spring*. New York: Fawcett, 1962.

Cheney, Jim, "Eco-feminism and deep ecology." *Environmental Ethics* (Summer 1987):115–145.

Clark, M. E. *Ariadne's thread*. New York: St. Martin's Press, 1989.

Clark, W. C. "Managing planet earth." *Scientific American* 261 (September 1989):3, 47–54.

Clarke, L. *Acceptable risk*. Berkeley, CA: University of California Press, 1990.

Commoner, Barry. *Making peace with the planet*. New York: Pantheon, 1990.

Cooperrider, D. L., and D. Billimoria. "The challenge of global change for strategic management." In P. Shrivastava, A. Huff, and J. Dutton, eds., *Advances in strategic management*, Vol. 9. Greenwich, CT: JAI Press, 1993.

Costanza, R. *Ecological economics*. New York: Columbia University Press, 1992.

Cote, R. "The industrial park as an ecosystem: managing for environmentally sustainable economic development." Brochure. Dartmouth, Nova Scotia: Dalhousie University, 1992.

Couch, S., and S. Kroll-Smith. *Communities at risk*. New York: Peter Lang, 1991.

Council on Environmental Quality. Total quality environmental management. Washington, DC: CEQ, 1993.

Daly, H. E. *Steady state economics*. New York: W. H. Freeman, 1977.

Daly, H. E. *Economics, ecology and ethics: essays toward a steady state economy*. Covello, CA: Island Press, 1980.

Daly, H. E. "Toward some operational principles of sustainable development." *Ecological Economics* 2 (1990):1–6.

Daly, H., and J. Cobb. *For the common good*. Boston: Beacon Press, 1989.

David, F. "How companies define their mission." *Long Range Planning* 22 (1989):15–24.

Davis, J. *Greening business*. Oxford, England: Basil Blackwell, 1991.

Devall, B., and G. Session. *Deep ecology: living as if nature mattered*. Layton, UT: Gibbs M. Smith Books, 1985.

Dicken, P. *Global shift: the internationalization of economic activity*. London: Paul Chapman, 1992.

Dobson, Andrew. *Green political thought*. London: Unwin Hyman, 1990.

Dogan, Mattie, and John D. Kasarda. *The metropolis era, Vol. 2*. Thousand Oaks, CA: Sage, 1988.

Douglas, Mary, and Aaron Wildavsky, *Risk and culture*. Berkeley, CA: University of California Press, 1982.

Durning, A. T. *How much is enough?* London: Earthscan, 1992.

Dutton, J. "Corporate citizenship at Merck: 'Good' to the core." Working Paper, Graduate School of Business, University of Michigan, 1992.

Ehrenfeld, D. *The arrogance of humanism*. Oxford, England: Oxford University Press, 1978.

Ehrlich, P., and A. Ehrlich. *The population explosion*. New York: Simon & Schuster, 1990.

EPA. *Environmental investments: The cost of a clean environment*. Washington, DC: U.S. Government Printing Office, 1990.

Environmental Defense Fund and McDonald's Corporation. *Waste reduction task force final report*. Washington, DC: Environmental Defense Fund, April, 1991.

Erikson, K. T. "Toxic reckoning." *Harvard Business Review* 90 No. 1 (1990):118–126.

Etzioni, A. *The moral dimension*. New York: Free Press, 1988.

Fischer, F. "Risk assessment and environmental crises: Toward integration of science and participation." *Industrial Crisis Quarterly* 5, No. 2 (1991).

Fischer, K., and J. Schot. *Environmental strategies for industry: International perspectives on research needs and policy implications.* Covello, CA: Island Press, 1993.

Freeman, E. *Strategic management: A stakeholder approach.* Boston: Pitman, 1984.

French, Hillary. "Green revolutions: Environmental reconstruction in Eastern Europe and the Soviet Union." Worldwatch Paper 99. Washington, DC: Worldwatch Institute, 1990.

Frosch, R. A., and N. E. Gallopoulos. "Strategies for manufacturing." *Scientific American* 261 (August 1989): 144–152.

Frost, P., et al. *Organizational culture.* Thousand Oaks, CA: Sage, 1985.

Fuwa, K. "History of Japan's industrial and environmental crises." *Industrial and Environmental Crisis Quarterly* 8, No. 2 (1994).

Gallup International Institute. Survey of environmental attitudes. Princeton, NJ: Gallup International Institute, 1992.

Garelik, G. "The Soviets clean up their act." *Time* (29 January 1990):64.

George, Susan. *How the other half dies.* New York: Penguin, 1976.

Giddens, A. *The consequences of modernity.* Palo Alto: Stanford University Press, 1990.

Giddens, A. *Modernity and self identity in the late modern age.* Cambridge, England: Cambridge University Press, 1991.

Gladwin, T. N. *Building the sustainable corporation: creating environmental sustainability and competitive advantage.* Washington: National Wildlife Federation, 1992.

Gladwin, T. N. "The meaning of greening: a plea for organizational theory." In K. Fischer, and J. Schot, *Environmental strategies for industry: international perspectives on research needs and policy implications.* Covello, CA: Island Press, 1993.

Goldsmith, Edward, and Nicholas Hildyard, eds. *The earth report.* London: Mitchell Beazley, 1988.

Goldstein R. L., and J. K. Shorr. *Demanding democracy after Three Mile Island.* Gainesville, FL: University of Florida Press, 1991.

Gorbachev, M. Address to the global forum on environmental protection and development for survival. Moscow: January 1989.

Gore, A. *Earth in the balance.* New York: Houghton-Mifflin, 1992.

Gross, N. "The green giant? It may be Japan." *Business Week* (24 February 1992):74–75.

Hirschhorn, J. S., and K. U. Oldenburg. *Prosperity without pollution. The prevention strategy for industry and consumers.* New York: Van Nostrand Reinhold, 1991.

Hiskes, R. P. "The democracy of risk." *Industrial Crisis Quarterly,* 6, No. 3 (1992):259–278.

Hoffman, W., R. Fredrick, and E. Petry. *The corporation, ethics and the environment.* Westport, CT: Quorum Books, 1990.

Hopfenbeck, W. *The green management revolution: Lessons in environmental excellence.* Englewood Cliffs, NJ: Prentice Hall, 1993.

Huddle, N., and M. Reich. *Island of dreams: Environmental crisis in Japan.* Shenkman, 1987.

Hunt, C., and E. Auster. "Proactive environmental management: Avoiding the toxic trap." *Sloan Management Review* 31 (1990):7–18.

Hershkowitz, A. *Garbage management in Japan.* New York: INFORM, 1988.

Kasperson, R. E., J. X. Kasperson, C. Hohenemser, and R. W. Kates, with O. Svenson, eds. *Corporate management of health & safety hazards.* Boulder, CO: Westview Press, 1988.

Kasperson, R. E., and P. M. Stallen. *Communicating risk to the public.* Dordrecht, Holland: Kluwer Academic Press, 1991.

Kirkpatrick, David. "Environmentalism: the crusade." *Fortune* (12 February):44–51.

Kleiner, A. "What does it mean to be green?" *Harvard Business Review* 69 (1991):38–47.

Kneese, A., and C. Schultze. *Pollution, prices, and public policy.* Washington, DC: The Brookings Institution, 1975.

Kolluru, R. V. *Environmental strategies handbook.* New York: McGraw-Hill, 1994.

Krimsky, S., and D. Golding. *Social theories of risk.* New York: Praeger, 1992.

Laird, F. "Technocracy revisited: knowledge, power, and the crisis in energy decision making." *Industrial Crisis Quarterly* 4, No. 1 (1990):49–61.

Landy, M., M. Roberts, and S. Thomas. *The Environmental Protection Agency: Asking the wrong questions.* Oxford, England: Oxford University Press, 1990.

Lash, S. "Reflexive modernization: the aesthetic dimension." *Theory, Culture, and Society* 10, No. 3 (1992).

Leopold, A. *A Sand County almanac*. New York: Oxford University Press, 1949.

Likens, G. "Chemical wastes in our atmosphere—an ecological crisis." *Industrial Crisis Quarterly* 1, No. 4 (1987):13–33.

Logsdon, J. *"Organizational responses to environmental issues: Oil refining companies and air pollution."* In L. E. Preston, ed., Research in corporate social performance and policy. Greenwich, CT: JAI Press, 1985.

Lovelock, J. "The greening of science." *Resurgence* 138 (1990):12–19.

———. *The ages of Gaia: A biography of our living earth*. New York: W. W. Norton, 1988.

Lovins, A. B. "The role of energy efficiency." In J. Leggett, ed., *Global warming: The Greenpeace report*. New York: Oxford University Press, 1990.

MacMillan, I. "Preemptive strategies." *Journal of Business Strategy* 4, No. 2 (1983).

MacNeil, J. "The greening of international relations." *International Journal* 24 (1989–90):1–35.

MacNeil, J., P. Winsemius and T. Yakushiji. Beyond interdependence. *Oxford, England: Oxford University Press, 1991.*

Makowver, J. *The E factor*. New York: Times Books, 1993.

Manes, C. *Green rage: radical environmentalism and the unmaking of civilization*. Boston: Little Brown, 1990.

Marshal, Patrick, "The greening of Eastern Europe." *The CQ Researcher* 1 (1991):26.

McGill, Douglas C. "Scour technology's stain with technology." *The New York Times Magazine* (4 October, 1992):32–60.

McGregor, Douglas. *The human side of enterprise*. New York: McGraw-Hill, 1960.

McGrew, T. "The political dynamics of the new environmentalism." *Industrial Crisis Quarterly* 4 (1990):291–306.

McKibben, R. *The end of nature*. New York: Random House, 1989.

McNeill, J. "Strategies for sustainable economic development." *Scientific American* 261 (September 1989):155–165.

Meadows, D. H., D. L. Meadows, and J. Randers. *Beyond the limits: confronting global collapse, envisioning a sustainable future*. Post Mills, VT: Chelsea Green, 1992.

Mercier, Michel, and Morrell Draper. "Chemical safety: The international outlook." *World Health* (August–September 1984).

Miller, D. *The Icarus paradox: How exceptional companies bring about their downfall.* New York: HarperCollins, 1990.

Mitroff, I. I., and R. H. Kilmann. *Corporate tragedies.* New York: Praeger, 1984.

——— and T. Pauchant. *We are so big and powerful, nothing bad can happen to us.* New York: Carol, 1990.

———, ——— and P. Shrivastava, "The structure of man-made organizational crises." *Technological Forecasting and Social Change* 33 (1988):83–107.

Morehouse, Ward, and Arun Subramaniam. *The Bhopal tragedy.* New York: Council on International and Public Affairs, 1988.

Naess, A. *Ecology, community and lifestyle: Ecosophy.* Cambridge, England: Cambridge University Press, 1987.

Nash, R. *The rights of nature.* Madison, WI: University of Wisconsin Press, 1989.

———. *Wilderness and the American mind.* New Haven, CT: Yale University Press, 1973.

Neeley, R. *The product liability mess.* New York: W. W. Norton, 1988.

Norris, R., A. Karim Ahmed, S. J. Sherr, and R. Richter. *Pills pesticides and profits: The international trade in toxic substances.* North River Press, 1982.

O'Connor, J. "Is sustainable capitalism feasible?" *Capitalism, Nature, Socialism,* 1991.

Orr, D. W. *Ecological literacy.* Buffalo, NY: State University of New York Press, 1992.

Ouchi, W. *Theory Z: How American business can meet the Japanese challenge.* Reading, MA: Addison-Wesley, 1981.

Pauchant, T., and J. Fortier. "Anthropocentric ethics in organizations, strategic management, and the environment." In P. Shrivastava and R. Lamb, eds., *Advances in Strategic Management,* Vol. 6. Greenwich, CT: JAI Press, 1990.

Pauchant, T., and I. Mitroff. "Crisis-prone versus crisis-avoiding organizations—Is your company's culture its own worst enemy in creating crises?" *Industrial Crisis Quarterly* 2 (1988):53–64.

Pearce, D. W., and R. K. Turner. *Economics of natural resources and the environment.* Baltimore, MD: Johns Hopkins Press, 1990.

Pearce, J., P. Loveridge, Tsurutani Taketsugu and Takematsu Abe. *Public knowledge and environmental politics in Japan and the United States.* Boulder, CO: Westview Press, 1989.

Perrow, C. *Normal accidents: Living with high risk technologies.* New York: Basic Books, 1984.

Picou, J. S., D .A. Gill, C. L. Dyer and E. N. Curry. "Disruption and stress in an Alaskan fishing community: initial and continuing impacts of the Exxon Valdez oil spill." *Industrial Crisis Quarterly* 6, No. 3 (1992):235–257.

Plotkin, G. "RATs to technology." *Industrial Crisis Quarterly* 3, No. 4 (1988).

Porter, M. *Competitive strategy.* New York: Free Press, 1980.

———. *Competitive advantage.* New York: Free Press, 1985.

———. *The competitive advantage of nations.* New York: Free Press, 1990.

Portney, K. E. *Siting hazardous waste treatment facilities: the NIMBY syndrome.* Auburn House, 1991.

Post, J. E. "Management as if the earth mattered." *Business Horizons* (1991).

Post, J., and B. Altman. "Corporate environmentalism: The challenge of organizational learning." Paper presented at the Academy of Management, August 12, 1991.

Postel, S. *Diffusing the toxics threat: Controlling pesticides and industrial wastes.* Worldwatch Paper 79, Washington, DC: Worldwatch Institute, 1987.

Prahalad, C. K., and G. Hamel. "The core competence of the corporation." *Harvard Business Review* (May–June 1990):79–91.

Preston, L., ed. *Research in corporate social performance.* Greenwich, CT: JAI Press, 1985.

Pryde, P. R. *Environmental management in the Soviet Union.* Cambridge, England: Cambridge University Press, 1991.

Quinn, R., and J. Rohrbaugh. "A spatial model of effectiveness criteria: Towards a competing values approach to organizational analysis." *Management Science* 29 (1983):363–377.

Redclift, M. *Sustainable development: Exploring the contradictions.* London: Methuen, 1989.

Reich, M. R. *Toxic politics: responding to chemical disasters.* Cornell University Press, 1991.

Repetto, R. *Promoting environmentally sound economic progress: What the north can do.* Washington, DC: World Resources Institute, 1990.

Renn, O. "Risk communication: towards a rational discourse with the public." *Journal of Hazardous Materials* (January 1992).

Roan, S. *The ozone crisis.* New York: Wiley, 1990.

Roddick, A. *Body and soul.* New York: Crown, 1991.

Rowland, F. S. "Can we close the ozone hole?" *Technology Review* 90, No. 6 (1987):50–58.

Ruckelshaus, W. "Toward a sustainable world." *Scientific American* 261 (September 1989):166–175.

Sadik, N. *The state of world population 1990.* New York: United Nations Population Fund, 1990.

Sale, K. *Human scale.* New York: Cowan, McCown, and Gesghyon 1986.

Schein, E. H. *Organization culture and leadership.* San Francisco: Jossey-Bass, 1985.

Schmidheiny, S. *Changing course: a global business perspective on development and the environment.* Cambridge: MIT Press, 1992.

Schnaiberg, A., N. Watts and K. Zimmerman, eds. *Distributional conflicts in environmental-resource policy.* Aldershot, England: Gower, 1986.

Schultze, C. *The public use of private interest.* Washington, DC: The Brookings Institution, 1977.

Schumacher, E. F. *Small is beautiful.* New York: Harper & Row, 1973.

Sethi, S. P. *Private enterprise and public purpose.* New York: Wiley, 1981.

———— and P. Steidelmeir. *Up against the corporate wall,* 5th ed. Englewood Cliffs, NJ: Prentice Hall, 1991.

Shimell, P. "Corporate environmental policy in practice." *Long Range Planning* 24 (1991):10–17.

Shiva, V. *Ecology and the politics of survival.* New Delhi: Sage, 1991.

Shrivastava, P. "Castrated environment: greening organizational studies." *Organization Studies* 15, No. 5 (1994):705–726.

————, "Ecocentric management in industrial ecosystems: management paradigm for a risk society." *Academy of Management Review* 20, (1995) forthcoming.

————, "Corporate self-greenewal: strategic responses to environmentalism." *Business Strategy and the Environment* 1, No. 3 (1992): 9–21.

————, *Bhopal: anatomy of a crisis.* London: Paul Chapman, 1992.

————, "Preventing industrial crises: the challenges of Bhopal." *International Journal of Mass Emergencies and Disasters* 5, No. 3 (1987):199–221.

————, and S. Hart. "Greening Organizations—2000." *International Journal of Public Administration* 17, Nos. 3 & 4 (1994):607–635.

————, "Ozone depletion crisis: A multiple stakeholder solution." *Business and Society Review* 75 (Fall 1990):59–62.

Siomkos, G. "Managing product harm crises." *Industrial Crisis Quarterly* 3, No. 1 (1989):41–60.

Slovic, P. "Perception of risk." *Science* (1987):280–285.

Slovic, P., B. Fischoff, and S. Lichtenstein. "Informing people about risk." In M. Mazis, L. Morris and B. Barofsky, eds., *Product labeling and health risks*. Bradbury Report 6. Cold Spring Harbor, NY Laboratory, 1980.

Smart, B., ed. *Beyond compliance: A new industry view of the environment*. Washington, DC: World Resources Institute, 1992.

Smith, Denis. *Business and the environment*. London: Paul Chapman, 1991.

Starik, M., and C. Gribbon. "European strategic environmental management: Toward a global model of business environmentalism." Paper presented at the IABS Annual Meeting, Leuven, Belgium, June 1992.

Stead, W., and J. Stead. *Management for a small planet*. Thousand Oaks, CA: Sage, 1992.

Stern, P. C., O. Young and D. Druckmann, eds. *Global environmental change: understanding the human dimensions*. National Research Council, National Academy Press, Washington, DC, 1992.

Svenson, Ola. "Managing product hazards at Volvo Car Corporation." In R. E. Kasperson, J. X. Kasperson, C. Hohenemser and R. W. Kates, eds., *Corporate management of health and safety hazards*. Boulder, CO: Westview Press, 1988.

Tibbs, H. *Industrial ecology: An environmental agenda for industry*. Arthur D. Little, 1991.

Tichy, Noel M. *Managing strategic change: technical, political and cultural dynamics*. New York: Wiley, 1983.

"Our fragile earth: IBM and the environment." *Think Magazine* 2 (1990).

Throop, G., M. Starik and G, Rands. "Strategic management in a greening world." In P. Shrivastava, A. Huff, and J. Dutton, eds., *Advances in strategic management, vol. 9*, Greenwich, CT: JAI Press, 1993.

Tolba, M. "Keynote speech to Globe 90." Address given at GLOBE '90, in Vancouver, BC, April 1990:19–23.

Turner, B. L. II et al. *The earth as transformed by human action*. Cambridge, England: Cambridge University Press, 1990.

Ui, Jun, ed. *Industrial pollution in Japan*. Tokyo: United Nations University Press, 1992.

United Nations Environment Program. *Human development report 1991*. Oxford, England: Oxford University Press, 1991.

————, *Environmental data report, 1989–90*. Oxford, England: Basil Blackwell, 1989.

————, IEO. Companies' organization and public communication on environmental issues. *Technical Report Series 6*. Paris: UNEP Industry and Environment Office, 1991.

Vallette, Jim. *The international trade in waste: a Greenpeace inventory*. Washington, DC: Greenpeace, 1989.

Vitousek, P. M., P. R. Ehrlich, A. H. Ehrlich, and P. Matson. "Human appropriation of the product of photosynthesis." *Bioscience* 36, No. 6, (1986):368–373.

Waterman, R., and T. Peters. *In search of excellence*. New York: Harper & Row, 1982.

Webler, T., H. Rakel, and R. S. H. Ross. "A critical theoretic look at risk analysis." *Industrial Crisis Quarterly* 6 No. 1 (1992).

Weir, D. *The circle of poison*. San Francisco: Sierra Club Books, 1982.

Westley, F., and H. Vrendenburg. "Strategic bridging: The collaboration between environmentalists and business in the marketing of green products." *Journal of Applied Behavioral Science* 27, No. 1 (1991).

White, L. "Religion and the ecological crisis." *Science* 155 (10 March 1967):1203–207.

Wildavsky, A. *Searching for safety*. New Brunswick, NJ: Transaction Books, 1988.

Wilson, E. "Threats to biodiversity." *Scientific American* 261 (September 1989):108–116.

Wood, D. "Corporate social performance revisited." *Academy of Management Review* 16, No. 4 (1991):691–718.

World Bank. World development report 1992: *Development and the environment*. Oxford, England: Oxford University Press, 1992.

World Commission on Environment and Development. *Our common future*. Oxford, England: Oxford University Press, 1987.

World Conservation Union, United Nations Environment Program, and World Wildlife Fund. *Caring for the earth: A strategy for sustainable living*. Gland, Switzerland: IUCN, UNEP, WWF, 1991.

World Resources Institute. *World resources 1992–93: Towards sustainable development.* New York: Oxford University Press, 1992.

Zimmerman, R. *Governmental management of chemical risk.* Oakgrove, IL: Lewis, 1990.

Index